Self-Sufficiency
Spinning, Dyeing, & Weaving

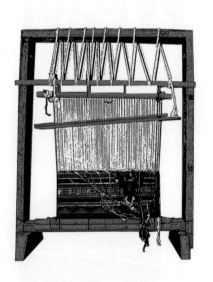

Self-Sufficiency

Spinning, Dyeing, & Weaving

Penny Walsh

Skyhorse Publishing

All Rights Reserved. No part of this book may be reproduced in any manner without the express written consent of the publisher, except in the case of brief excerpts in critical reviews or articles. All inquiries should be addressed to Skyhorse Publishing, 555 Eighth Avenue, Suite 903, New York, NY 10018.

Skyhorse Publishing books may be purchased in bulk at special discounts for sales promotion, corporate gifts, fund-raising, or educational purposes. Special editions can also be created to specifications. For details, contact the Special Sales Department, Skyhorse Publishing, 555 Eighth Avenue, Suite 903, New York, NY 10018 or info@skyhorsepublishing.com.

www.skyhorsepublishing.com

10 9 8 7 6 5 4 3 2 1

Library of Congress Cataloging-in-Publication Data

Walsh, Penny.
  Spinning, dyeing, and weaving : self-sufficiency / Penny Walsh.
    p. cm.
  Includes index.
  ISBN 978-1-61608-002-0 (hardcover : alk. paper)
  1. Hand spinning. 2. Dyes and dyeing, Domestic. 3. Hand weaving. I. Title.
  TT847.W35 2010
  746.1'2—dc22
                          2009046856

Printed in China

CONTENTS

Introduction   6

Fiber   8
Combing and carding   30
Spinning   42
Dyeing   58
Weaving   86
Projects   110

Resources   121
Glossary   123
Index   125
Acknowledgments   127

Introduction

With the mighty textile industry able to produce cloth more quickly than ever before, and stores selling furnishing and clothing textiles in every town center, why engage in the labor-intensive and time-consuming process of making your own textiles? The answer is that there are so many mass-produced and easily available inexpensive furnishings and clothing that our reaction is to want something different, and indeed nothing could be more different from modern factory-made cloth than unique handmade textiles. Moreover, although manufactured textiles employ some of the most sophisticated techniques of any modern industry, the entire production method can also be done by hand, using almost no energy but your own.

Producing homemade textiles

If you are serious about being fully self-sufficient in making your own textiles, you have to take spinning, dyeing, and weaving right back to where almost no power, except people power, is used. Additionally, all fibers and colors should be sourced as locally and cheaply as possible, and the coloring processes should be carried out using little or no heat. Surprisingly, even making reasonably large textile pieces can be done in the home, using ordinary domestic equipment. The fabrics produced using these methods will be quite different in feel, behavior, color, and durability from machine-made textiles, and, with the right care, handmade textiles will age gracefully and last forever!

Handmaking methods are very time-consuming, and it is almost impossible to be completely self-sufficient in all textile needs; some machine-made textiles are simply a necessity in the 21st century. But the actual process of making materials offers more than just the end product; the time taken to create a piece is more than repaid by the relish and delight of the creative process. The repetitive rhythms of spinning and weaving are absorbing and (except when something goes wrong) very soothing.

Aims of the book

In order to work towards finished textiles that are both useful and beautiful, and can be made from scratch at home, this book covers all areas of the textile-making process: from fiber combing and carding, to spinning, dyeing, and weaving. This allows the complete beginner to work through them all, and allows more experienced practitioners to try out new areas.

The book will show how to get hold of the fibers to spin into yarns and source them inexpensively, either by growing them from seed or obtaining them from animals. It will then cover the preparatory processes for spinning yarns and reveal the various shortcuts and tricks of the trade to make the resulting yarn a much higher quality. This is followed by an explanation of how to spin the prepared fibers on a drop spindle and then on a spinning wheel to produce yarns that are specifically designed for a particular project.

Dyeing yarn follows, using natural dyestuffs and assistants from the garden or kitchen, and employing techniques that require the least amount of energy to produce good, viable colors. The dyed handspun yarn can then be woven on a variety of devices, from a simple frame or card, to a large rug or tapestry frame.

In the chapter on weaving, we will look at the methods of constructing a simple loom or frame, and how to make a range of textiles that can be woven using them. From these basics, more complicated pattern weaves, requiring a professionally-made loom, can be understood.

Four projects round off the book, so that you can put into practice all that you have learned!

Fiber

At the heart of all natural textiles are fibers. Many people source them from suppliers, but you can also produce your own. This chapter shows the variety of animals and vegetables that can be used for fiber, plus how you can both produce and source your materials to create your own textiles.

Producing your own fleece

A couple of sheep, alpacas, or Angora goats kept in a small paddock or uncultivated area of your garden can provide large quantities of fleece—as well as the company of friendly pets. Much happier and no more trouble in pairs than on their own, their dainty hooves will improve the soil and they will need very little hands-on looking after, as they are easy to care for and hardy in winter. Angora rabbits need even less space and, although needing rather more specialized care, will grow considerable amounts of a seriously luxurious fiber.

Sheep
Sheep can be bought at markets, from local breeders, or farms. Different sheep breeds have different wool, so you will need to obtain a breed suitable for hand spinning (see pages 44–9). A good way of obtaining a specific breed of sheep is to find a local breeder and buy lambs or young sheep from them (the fleece of sheep up to four years old is of a much higher quality than that of older sheep). Often, these small flocks are bred by people who understand wool quality, and even the least perfect lambs will give you wonderful wool.

Approximately ⅓ acre will give two sheep enough year-round grazing space—they will need a constant supply of grass during the year and they will also need to be fenced in. Sheep eat many kinds of weeds and keep pretty healthy (especially when kept in small numbers). They will be gentle, good company, and sociable. Sheep are shorn once a year in late spring. Management and preparation of the fleece varies from breed to breed and is dealt with in the Spinning chapter (see pages 42–57).

Angora goats

Angora goats grow a long, curling, shiny coat that can be spun into mohair yarn. They originate in Turkey and Central Asia, and "mohair" is a translation of a word that means "best fleece." Slightly more tricky to rear than sheep, they will repay their owner with mounds of lustrous yarn that is soft and, if carefully managed, has none of the prickliness of some commercial mohair garments.

There are a few established herds to buy from, and ¼ acre is sufficient space for two animals (it is cruel to keep a solitary animal). Angora goats will munch their way through weeds, shrubs, and nettles, but will need some food supplements in winter. Unlike sheep, they will also need some shelter in the winter months and after shearing if the weather is still cold.

The Angora goat grows fleece at a phenomenal speed (1 in. per month) and a six-month fleece is the ideal length for a hand spinner. After shearing, the fleece can be rather waxy so it will need washing in soap suds and drying before spinning, taking care not to disturb the parallel fibers in each lock.

Cashmere goats

Producing fleece from the truly legendary Cashmere goat is problematic for the self-sufficient textile maker because the goats are difficult to rear away from their cold, dry homeland and only produce small amounts of fiber. Unsurprisingly, the finest cashmere is still only found in Kashmir and the surrounding Asiatic countries like Tibet, Mongolia, China, and Afghanistan. To avoid the blunt ends that shearing entails, the goats are not shorn; instead, the superfine fiber is combed from the fleeces at molting time by the shepherds. Though the coats of locally-bred Cashmere goats are a little thicker than those of their Asiatic relatives, their fleece is still fine and very soft. Cashmere goats are medium-size and very hardy. When combed or clipped, each fleece weighs around 2–4.5 lbs. and will not need sorting as it is fairly uniform in length and will just need a light wash.

Alpacas

These camelids are slightly larger than goats and originate from South America, where their fleeces were used by the Incas who bred them for fine and colored fleeces. Easy to feed, they will browse on shrubs, grass, and hay. They are very resistant to cold, but not so much to rain, as their fleece has no protective lanolin so they will need shelter. They can be shorn once a year in late spring and the fleece can weigh up to 6 lbs. 10 oz., although this can be much less in young animals.

Huaca alpacas give larger fleeces but the Suri fleece is the silkiest of all. The fleece will not need heavy washing and is of fairly uniform length. Alpacas are alert and inquisitive, and enjoy going for walks on a leading reign, which may surprise the neighbors!

Angora rabbits

Prize-winning Angora rabbits look like big balls of floating thistledown, from which an incredibly cute bunny-rabbit face looks out, surmounted by huge, soft, furry ears—with tassels on the ends in some breeds. Angora rabbits produce more high-quality and valuable fleece for the amount of food and space they take up than any other animal but the hand spinner and weaver should be cautious as experienced care and expertise are required to successfully harvest the fleeces.

Although these rabbits are usually calm, docile, and seem to enjoy petting and handling, they have to be groomed every day when they are in full fleece or they will fall prey to hairballs and tangling, which can eventually immobilize them. Caring for the rabbits and their fleece is really only for the enthusiast, and, although I have known textile artists who have successfully completed the whole process—from rearing, plucking, or shearing the fleece, to spinning, knitting, and weaving beautiful angora garments—I have also known of many long-haired rabbits brought to be re-homed. Once the fleece has been clipped, however, it is comparatively trouble-free as it does not require much washing or sorting and can be laid in a box with the cut ends at one end, ready to spin.

The hair should be spun very finely or mixed with fine, soft wool like merino, and sometimes silk—so a little goes a long way (see page 54 for further details).

Dogs
This type of animal hair is very dear to some and it is unlikely that anybody would keep a dog just for the fiber. There are many people who have been delighted with sweaters made from their own Old English sheepdogs. Dogs with long, fine fur provide the most suitable hair for hand spinning—principally the Samoyed and Chow breeds, but, surprisingly, good results have also been achieved using fur from Alsatians and Collies, especially when they are blended with other fibers.

It is vital that dog hair is thoroughly washed before spinning preparation or the dog is thoroughly washed before its hair is clipped.

Cats
Obtaining fleece from cats is almost impossible due to the nature of the fur (and the animal!). Most cat hair is straight and shiny, without any torque, so even the longer hairs will slide out of a yarn. A minimal amount of fleece can, however, be obtained from Persian and Angora breeds, but there is always a lingering aroma of cat, which is not always desirable!

Silkworms
Rearing silkworms provides valuable fiber for very little expenditure as well as a fascinating experience. They can be kept in plastic fish tanks with only twigs for furniture. However, as with Angora rabbits, rearing them is not to be undertaken unless you are prepared to make this into an activity you can give some time to as they grow quickly and consume huge quantities of leaves, so will need feeding several times a day. When

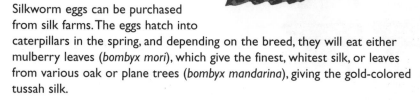

they start spinning
the gossamer silk for their
cocoons, they stop
eating and will not need
feeding again as once they have
spun their cocoon, they sit in it,
hatch, lay eggs, and die.

Silkworm eggs can be purchased
from silk farms. The eggs hatch into
caterpillars in the spring, and depending on the breed, they will eat either
mulberry leaves (*bombyx mori*), which give the finest, whitest silk, or leaves
from various oak or plane trees (*bombyx mandarina*), giving the gold-colored
tussah silk.

Six to eight weeks after hatching they will spin on average 295 to 330 feet of
silk into a cocoon before laying eggs and dying. For the animal lovers among
you, the advantage of keeping your own worms
is that you can allow the cocoons to pupate
and the moths to hatch (commercially, the
larvae are killed so that the cocoons remain
unbroken). There are now some companies
advertising "veggie" silk, or silk without
cruelty—unraveled silk from broken cocoons from
which the moths have been allowed to emerge.

Growing your own vegetable fibers

Fiber can also be obtained from plants. A fairly small patch, around 32 square feet, is all you need to grow enough plants to yield sufficient fiber to make a throw, or a scarf or two. However, the rather lengthy harvesting and preparation processes make this a less financially and economically viable option than obtaining fiber from animals, in that only relatively small amounts of fiber can be harvested within the confines of your garden whereas animals provide masses of fleece for little effort.

Linen

Flax (*Linum usitatissimum*) is one of the oldest known crops and has been grown as two varieties, one for fiber and one for linseed oil, since the Stone Age. The fiber flax is a tall variety with no branches and the strong, woody, or "bast," fibers are in the stem.

To grow enough flax to yield a viable amount of fiber, you will need around 21.5 square feet of land—a small allotment or large flowerbed is ideal. The closer together the seeds are sown, the finer the quality of the fiber bundles will be, so sowing up to 3,000 plants per 10 square feet is the norm. Smaller areas of flax for hand spinning should be sown thickly in slightly acidic soil early in the year, from late February to early April, so that they don't grow too rapidly and weaken the fibers.

Harvesting linen is done by pulling, not cutting, as the roots are short and contain the ends of the fibers.

The plants should be pulled in July when the lower two-thirds of the stem has turned yellow. If the flax is allowed to mature fully, the fibers will be stiff and coarse, and more difficult to work with. Once pulled the flax should be tied in bundles and left to dry.

Hemp

Hemp (*Cannabis sativa*) was widely grown in Europe from 800 to 1800, and has recently attracted the attention of sustainable farmers as it needs little water, renitrogenates the soil, and has a much larger yield per yard than linens. The fibers have anti-mildew properties and are also believed to possess antimicrobial properties. Additionally, hemp seed oil is anti-inflammatory.

Hemp grows vigorously in most soils, although it dislikes dry, sandy conditions. Sprouted seedlings should be planted in early April to early May, 4½ in. apart and at a depth of 1½ in. As with flax, an area of 21½ square feet should give enough yield to be usable. Hemp is resistant to disease and weeds, and will form a dense canopy. After 13 to 14 weeks, when a few leaves drop from the stems, it should be pulled up in small handfuls, tied in bundles, and laid to dry for four days.

Nettle fiber

The common nettle (*Urtica doica*) is a subject of great interest to the textile industry. Its cousin ramie (*Boehmeria nivea*) has been successfully farmed for several years and is now a regular constituent in high-street clothing. Even the nettles in our garden have potential as a fiber crop. Stronger than cotton and finer (although shorter) than linen, nettle fiber was used in Scotland until the 17th century

for household linens (known as "napery"). Nettles can also be used as a dye, to make paper, and even as a foodstuff. It seems unnecessary to discuss how to grow nettles as they grow rampantly and are considered weeds. Once cut, mature nettles should be steeped in water and dried. However hard you try and however thick your gardening gloves, you will always get stung (though painful, this is now thought to be extremely beneficial for rheumatic and arthritic conditions!).

Recycled fibers

Recycled fibers used to be very big business. Until the early 1970s, "shoddy" mills in Yorkshire efficiently shredded wool rags and turned old socks and blankets into fibers that could be re-combed to spin into wool yarns. In the 1860s, Batley in Yorkshire boasted thirty shoddy mills, making it the center of the industry. In the United States there are still a couple of surviving mills in Newark.

Recycling fibers is an appealing idea to the self-sufficient spinner but it is not so straightforward. The shoddy mills used extremely heavy machinery to shred the rags for recycling. On a small scale, it is possible to re-card loosely woven or knitted fabrics with a drum carder (see pages 39–40). It is also possible to reuse chopped, re-twisted soft cotton or wool yarns to re-spin or for decorative effects. And, of course, the self-sufficient weaver can use recycled yarns unraveled from all manner of sweaters and loosely knitted textiles.

Sourcing and choosing wool and fleeces

When it comes to selecting and obtaining fibers for spinning, most hand spinners think of wool. Sheep's wool or fleece is by far the easiest fiber to hand spin because of its elasticity, crimp, and curl. Knitters and weavers love it for its versatility, softness, resilience, and warmth.

Sheep fleece is easily obtained in large quantities, often at low prices and sometimes even for free from the following sources:

• **Wool dealers.** There are more than thirty dealers who buy wool in the United States. The American Sheep Industry Association is a great resource to finding wool dealers around the country. Visit www.sheepusa.org/Wool_Contacts for more information. Some wool dealers even have a little shop area and sell other sheep-related items. This really is the next best thing to keeping your own sheep as you will be spinning inspected and valued fleece from the sheep in your local area.

• **Craft suppliers.** This is a more commercial way to purchase fleece. Some textile suppliers will sell and even post raw fleece to hand spinners, and you will find that you get a lot of fleece for your money. There are many advantages to this: The fleece has usually had the worst of the muck shaken out of it and you will probably get sent the best pieces of fleece. Very often, the suppliers understand hand spinning and will offer help and advice, and you can get the variety and color you want.

• **Rare breed farms.** As farmers have diversified, many of them have started rearing flocks of rare breed sheep for specialized meats or simply to attract tourists. There are also rare breed survival centers. Very interesting fleeces can be bought at farm open days for very little, but caution is advised. "Rare" does not necessarily mean suitable for hand spinning. These sheep are not bred specifically by wool specialists and may not be cared for in the right way before and after shearing to produce a fleece fit for spinning. I have bought some fabulous fleeces but in some cases the fleece has been disappointing, sometimes because the open day or sale is long after shearing and the fleeces have been squashed into unsuitable bags and stored in dusty barns for too long.

- **Sheep and wool festivals**. These festivals are a great way of seeing fleeces "on the hoof" and to meet farmers or owners of small flocks of the types of sheep suitable for hand spinning. Festivals are advertised on the Internet, in sheep-related magazines and spinning journals, or by contacting agricultural colleges.

- **eBay**. A surprising number of fleeces are offered on eBay. However, do bear in mind that you are buying without handling, and unlike the craft supplier there won't be the advice or the opportunity to obtain sample packs. Remember that even part of a fleece, because of its bulk, is quite awkward to deal with or re-pack if it is unsatisfactory and needs to be returned.

- **Gifts**. Beware of friends bearing fleeces! Or friends offering fleeces on behalf of their friends, and neighbors who "keep a few sheep." The sheep may have wool that resembles barbed wire! If you reveal yourself to be hand spinning your own wool, everyone will know a friendly farmer who has a barn full of fleeces that he is willing to give away. In moderation, this can be a wonderful opportunity, but make sure you don't accept more than one fleece at a time as they take up a lot of space and may not be of good enough quality for spinning. Be wary and make tactful enquiries before committing yourself.

Which fleece?

There are hundreds of different breeds of sheep, but because the historic wool industry of the British Isles stretches back to the Iron Age, they produce more sheep and types of wool than anywhere else in the world. These British breeds were selectively bred and exported in the 19th and 20th centuries to many other wool-producing areas, very often in combination with the Spanish merino—a descendent of the extinct Roman merino—the sheep that produced the finest wool ever spun.

There are about forty different pure breeds in the British Isles and around 200 half-breeds and crossbreeds recognized worldwide. For instance, the Australian Corriedale is a crossbreed of merino and Lincoln, and the American Columbia sheep is a crossbreed of Leicester and French Rambouillet (a fine wool merino descendent). All fleece sheep are divided into three main categories:

• **Mountain and moorland sheep.** These have coarse fleeces and include Scottish Blackface, Cheviot, Swaledale, and Herdwick. They are independent and strong with an endearing hefting instinct that will attach a flock forever to its hill or mountain.

• **Longwool and luster breeds.** These include Lincoln Longwool, Wensleydale, Romney, Black Welsh Mountain, and Teeswater. Big sheep with long curling fleeces, the Lincoln and Romney have lived in damp marshy pastures for 700 or 800 years and form the basis of countless other crossbreeds.

• **Shortwool and downland breeds.** Dense, soft fleeces of manageable length make the sheep in this category the favorite with hand spinners. They include the Hampshire Down, Oxford Down, Southdown, Ryland (famous for its high quality fleece), and the Shetland.

The last two categories are suitable for hand spinning for clothing. The mountain and moorland fleeces are used for rugs and carpets and are rarely hand spun, although flocks within these wide categories will vary. For instance, some Cheviot and Herdwick fleeces can be strong and crisp but also soft, and some Black Welsh Mountain fleeces are soft enough for drapey throws or jackets.

Beginners should use a shortwool or downland breed. Romney or Southdown have open fleeces that are easy to sort but with enough crimp to give them an inclination to twist and ply.

For a lustrous, smooth yarn for weaving, longwool and luster breeds can be combed to spin into smooth, shiny yarn. Too heavy for undergarments, the yarn will be suitable for jackets, hats, and wraps, and excellent for throws. These fleeces are more suitable for experienced spinners as their length makes them difficult to spin.

For soft, woollen sweaters and scarves, the downland breeds have a high density of fine fibers and will easily spin into a soft, "lofty" (fluffy) thread. Beginners will find a medium-fine Suffolk or Kent fleece straightforward to spin up for knitting yarn. The superfine merino and fine Shetland fleeces are tricky to work with and best reserved for more experienced spinners. They are ideal for making the sorts of yarn suitable for "heirloom" christening shawls and "ring" shawls (shawls that are fine enough to pass through a wedding ring).

What to look for in a fleece

After you have decided what sort of fleece you want and the most cost-effective way to obtain it, you will need to make sure that the fleece under consideration is suitable for your purposes.

You can test the quality of the fleece in the following ways:

1) **Unrolling it**. If the fleece is rolled up, as it often is after shearing, you should unroll it to ensure that it has been rolled in the correct way, with the euphemistically-termed "skirtings" (the soiled areas) on the outside. If the fleece has been rolled up with damp or manure-covered bits in the middle of the roll it may be unusable, since soaking manure out is not a pleasant job and it can permanently stain the wool.

2) **Checking the condition**. Look at the general condition of the fleece and see if it is matted, damp, or too dry. You should look for any earth, sand, or straw enmeshed in the wool, which can make the process of spinning impossible. Excessive staining may not wash out of a white fleece, and the tips of a colored fleece may be so weathered that they have faded to a different color.

3) **Looking for "kemp."** This term refers to the thick, white, springy hairs that can develop in a fleece. Some breeds are more prone to developing kemp than others. It is a feature of Harris Tweed cloth—think of the bristly white hairs that stick out of grandpa's tweed jacket. But unless you are weaving your own Harris Tweed, a kempy fleece is to be avoided as it is stiff and prickly and will not take any dye.

4) **Measuring the staple length**. Take out one staple or lock of wool from the middle of the best part of the fleece and measure its length; this is referred to as the "staple length." The very longest can measure 12 in., and

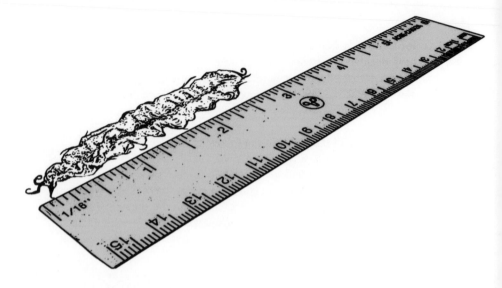

the shortest can be 1½–2 in. As a beginner, you will probably want something that is around 3¼ in.

5) **Checking the thickness.** Look closely at the thickness of each fiber and decide if the fibers are the right thickness for your purpose. The thickness of wool is measured as a "count," with a lower count of 25–30 being a very coarse fleece, like Cheviot or Herdwick, and a higher count of over 60 being a very fine fleece, like merino. A medium fleece, like Oxford Down, has a count of 55.

6) **Examining the crimp.** Next, look at the amount of crimp or wave (also known as character) along the length of the staple. The crimp is what makes sheep's wool different from other animals'—being warm, resilient, and uniquely suitable for spinning. For beginners, the more crimp, the better; for experienced spinners, the crimp should be just enough for the sort of twist you want to put in.

7) **Pulling it.** Take both ends of the staple and tug a few times, then look carefully at the middle of the staple: If the sheep has had a hard winter or early lambs, the center of the staple may be weak and may break under pressure. This is known as a "tender" fleece and is low quality so you shouldn't buy it.

Sorting

Having found a source of fleece and chosen one, you may feel a little intimidated by how enormous it looks spread out. Commercially, fleeces are sorted into several grades of wool, depending on the breed. In fact, some breeds grow a uniform length of fleece over the whole body.

For the hand spinner, it is usually enough to sort into three parts: the very dirty/short/discolored "skirtings" that may either be soaked and felted, or discarded to use in the garden; then two grades of wool—one bag of clean, uniform length, dense and longish wool, usually from the shoulders and back, and one bag of uneven length, matted and shorter wool from the rump, head, and tummy. Smaller fleeces like Shetland don't need sorting.

Scouring

This is one of the most important processes in preparing a fleece to spin, and surprisingly it is optional! Most hand spinners prefer to spin fleece "in the grease," or just as it came off the sheep. They find that it does not suffer stretching and breaking during the carding and spinning processes, and that it spins more easily and washes better as yarn. But if the fleece is "sticky" or if you just can't handle unwashed fleece, then a soak is all that is needed to clean it at this stage.

Divide the fleece into sections as it will be too large to handle in one piece, then soak overnight in the bath in tepid water. The next day, lift it out of the bath, taking care not to squeeze or twist it. Transfer into another bath of clean, tepid water, pressing down on the fleece with the palms of your hands, then lift out. Do not squeeze the fleece; instead, drain and dry it on a flat surface.

Sourcing, choosing, and preparing other animal fibers

Angora goats (mohair)

Angora goats have been farmed since the beginning of the 20th century in the United States, Australia, and South Africa. Prize-winning billy goats cost literally thousands of dollars and there is a limited number of farmers selling fleeces for hand spinning. They can be contacted at shows and by visiting the farms. As Angoras are reared for their fleece only and there is no income from meat, the farmers have to rely on the beauty and charm of the animals to attract visitors, so they are often easy to locate and visit. Because the fleeces are large with little waste, they make an enormous amount of yarn, so that even the cost of a pedigree fleece is negligible if you are going to make your own textiles.

Shearing takes place twice a year, in early spring and early autumn. The best, or "diamond," fleeces are graded by their luster, which is a result of the surface of the fiber being much flatter than that of wool and therefore reflecting the light more. Fleeces are also graded according to length, with the average being 4 in. when straightened out.

Additionally, fleeces are also graded according to the age of the animal. Kid mohair (6–12 months), young goat (18–24 months), and adult (30+ months). Mohair becomes coarser as the goat gets older but after 4 or 5 years it remains constant. Other than knowing the age and background of the animal, the spinner can only rely on their hands and eyes to choose a good one. To check the fleece, part the locks right down to the bottom and look at the luster—don't be put off by dull or greasy looking locks at the top as the natural oils will wash out easily.

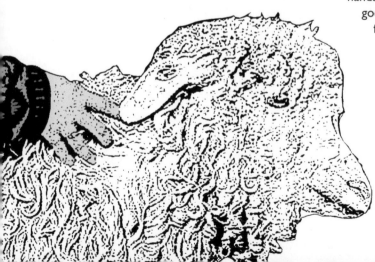

Look out for kemp down the back of the fleece—Angora goats can have it, too, although breeders are trying (and succeeding) in eliminating the brittle kempy hairs.

Tight ringlets and lots of "character" (waves and curls), usually indicate the finest fleeces, with fibers 20–40 microns thick (the human hair averages 60 microns). Sorting is not relevant, as when shorn, the locks do not stay in a fleece like sheep's wool; instead each staple falls loose, so it is only necessary to remove the soiled bits for soaking.

Cashmere goats

Finding a fleece is not easy. In fact, in the UK the only cashmere farmers are in Scotland. There are many in the United States and Australia, but they probably all have their fleeces prepared and spun by mills, and don't have any left for hand spinners (however it might be worth asking). If they do sell fleece, it will not be cheap and they may wish to sell a minimum of 11 lbs. It is easier to buy prepared fleece in a combed sliver. If you do get the chance to obtain a fleece, it should already be de-haired—the cashmere is usually shorn by combing the molting fine hairs and leaving the guard hairs on the goat. However, if the guard hairs are left in the fleece they need to be lightly combed out (see spinning preparation section on pages 30–41).

The only way to decide on fleece quality is by feel. High-quality cashmere has an indefinable soft, slippery feel because of the extreme fineness of the fibers (they average 18–19 microns, one-third of a human hair!). The fleeces should be relatively clean, as Cashmere goats produce dry pellets. The only sorting that may be necessary will be to look for food contamination if the goats have been fed from a high feeder.

Alpacas

The glamorous alpaca is not related to the sheep or goat and consequently has a very different fleece. Soft and light, it is generally described as a wool but contains no lanolin or grease so it does not need washing (although alpacas love dustbaths so the wool may need a good shake). The fleece is made up of hollow fibers with excellent thermal qualities. The few thick guard hairs that keep off the rain and protect the fine fleece among the soft coat have been almost eradicated by selective breeding and the large alpaca farms in the United States now produce very fine fleeces of 20–35 microns. In Peru, there are rumors of a 17-micron alpaca fleece!

Obtaining a prime alpaca fleece is still inexpensive. Fleeces can be bought from specialized farmers or at shows in the same way as mohair. They come in the largest range of colors of any natural fiber—twenty-two shades are recognized in Peru—which makes buying a fleece very exciting. Crimpiness and curl do vary from animal to animal and generally the more crimp, the better. When you have purchased your fleece, it will just need sorting into "prime" (mostly back and shoulders) and seconds (the rest).

A fine fleece will make two to three sweaters or a couple of large throws.

Angora rabbits

If you decide not to keep your own rabbits, the only way to obtain this fiber is from a breeder who is probably also a hand spinner. You can find breeders at fairs or shows or by contacting Angora rabbit societies. Angora is so fine and has no grease or other contamination so the only thing to look for in a fleece is to make sure it isn't tangled (the fine hairs can knit themselves into a solid felt if they are disturbed). The fleeces should be stored in parallel piles in a box or on a flat surface. They will probably have been sorted already, as any tangled or discolored fleece is not worth struggling with.

Silk

Silk can be bought from silk suppliers in a variety of forms. The silk filaments are reeled off the cocoons and the longest unbroken lengths are used to weave high-quality silk gauze. The rest is combed into long swathes and sold as slivers or compacted into silk "bricks." Hand spinners can also buy silk squares or "caps"; these are whole cocoons stretched out into squares or bell shapes.

Exotic animal fibers

There are no shortcuts to obtaining exotic animal fibers cheaply, but purchasing enough from a craft supplier or through the Internet to hand spin and weave is surprisingly economical. You can try zoos if you have a yearning for Canadian Musk Ox or Vicuna. Advertisements in specialist trade and craft magazines are also good sources.

Sourcing vegetable fibers

As these fibers are not farmed in many places (even the Irish and Belgian linen manufacturers are supplied by Asia) there are only two ways to obtain raw vegetable fibers: grow your own or buy them from a hand spinning supplier. Linen, cotton, ramie nettle, and hemp are all sold ready to spin in craft shops, but be aware that as they are derived from living plants they are not uniform. Linen fiber can be particularly variable in texture, and if not used within a year or so becomes brittle. Linen is measured in "lea"; the finest handkerchief fibers are 40 lea (12,000 yards per lb). Cotton is graded according to length, which depends on variety, the longest being Sea Island, followed by Egyptian, and then American. Indian cotton is too short to hand spin. As with linen, be careful when buying hemp and jutes: the fibers should be slightly glossy but soft and pliable, and not too thick to twist into a fine thread. It is always a good idea to handle a small twist of fiber before purchasing.

Waste fibers

Machine spinning processes result in a certain amount of waste fiber and both waste silk and cotton can be purchased from fiber suppliers or craft outlets. They cost next to nothing but are not really suitable to use on their own; however, they can make an interesting addition when spinning other fibers.

Combing and carding

Once you have chosen and obtained your fibers, you are ready to start on the real work. Fleeces will have been sorted and shaken out, and pet and rabbit hair will have been packed or boxed to keep it in order. Homegrown linen or hemp will have been harvested and ready for preparing. If you have bought prepared fibers, you are all ready to go! The four main processes covered in this chapter (teasing, combing, hand carding, and drum carding) work for wool and fleeces but also apply if you are mixing fibers.

Teasing

Teasing out fleece with your fingers can be a relaxing process, and is essential in familiarizing yourself with the characteristics of a fiber. By separating and arranging the wool or hair, and discarding weak or short bits, you can prepare the fiber for easy carding or combing. If you have a fleece that is clean and of an even consistency, you can spin it just after a light teasing. Traditional spinners of fine fleeces, like Shetland, maintain that the fleece is ruined and stretched by carding, and loudly proclaim that the lightest and finest yarn can only be spun from gently teased fleece.

Teasing out fiber

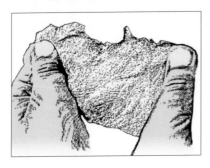

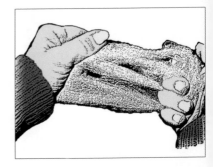

1) Take a handful of fibers and hold in both hands, thumb to thumb. Pull your hands apart sideways, then separate out one staple (or lock).

2) Hold the tip (the opposite end to the shorn or cut end) of the staple in one hand and gently pull at the other end, inserting your fingers into the fibers like a comb.

Staple length
At this point it is useful to establish the "staple length," or the average length, of the fibers you are dealing with. To do this, take a handful of fibers and pull them out, then measure them with a ruler (see pages 23–4).

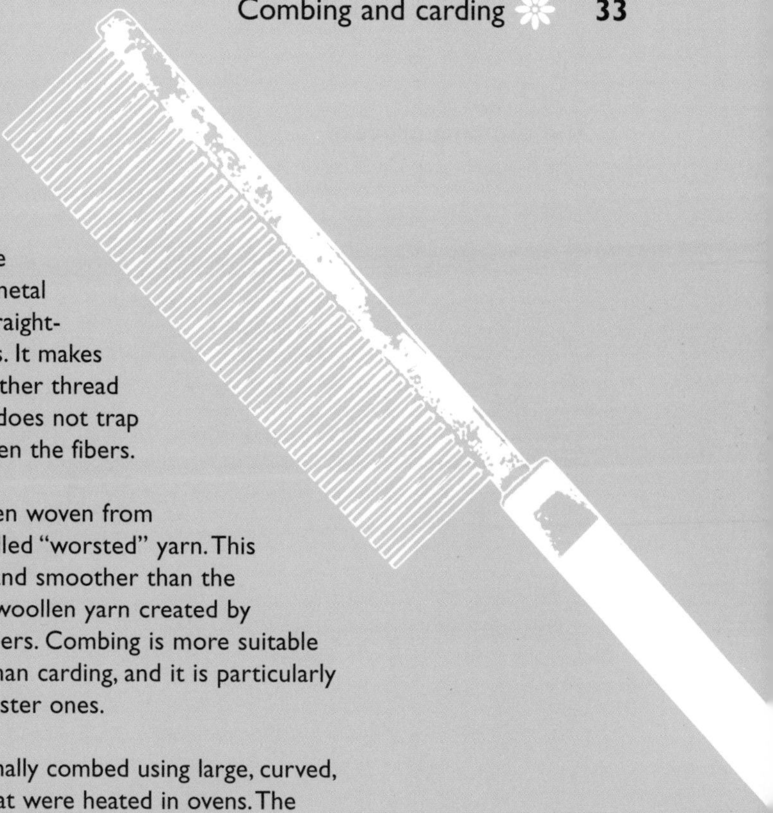

Combing

Combing wool
involves drawing
staples through the
tines (teeth) of a metal
comb to create straight-
ened, aligned fibers. It makes
a firmer and smoother thread
than carding, as it does not trap
as much air between the fibers.

Fabric that has been woven from
combed yarn is called "worsted" yarn. This
is much stronger and smoother than the
fabric made from woollen yarn created by
spinning carded fibers. Combing is more suitable
for longer fibers than carding, and it is particularly
suitable for high-luster ones.

Wool was traditionally combed using large, curved,
rake-like combs that were heated in ovens. The
work was hot and hard, and undertaken by
brawny men famous for the amounts of beer
they could drink to slake their fiendish thirsts!
The easiest way for the home spinner to
comb locks of fiber is with a dog comb,
which has rows of soft wire teeth, or
with any metal comb.

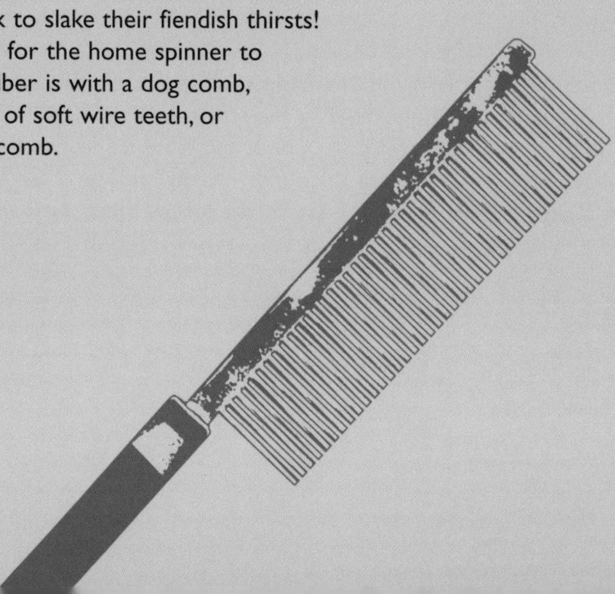

The combing process

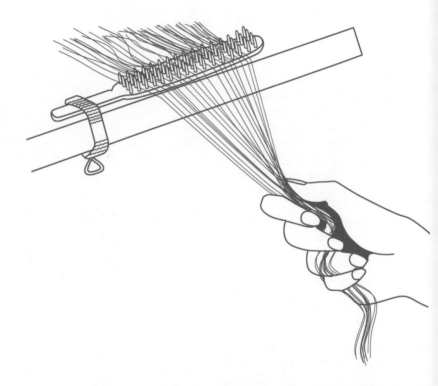

1) Hold the comb firmly in one hand or clamp it to a table if possible for very strong or sticky fibers. Holding the staple very tightly in the other hand, hook the tip of the staple onto the comb and draw it through the tines. When the fibers are released from the comb, "throw" (place) them back onto the tines slightly further down the staple, then draw them through the tines again.

2) Turn the staple round and draw the other end through the comb so that you are combing the end you were holding. This will result in a combed staple of parallel fibers, leaving some shorter hairs in the comb, which can be removed and carded (see page 36).

3) To complete the process, draw the combed staple out into a long sliver of parallel fibers by gently pulling it. This can be coiled into a basket or onto a tray so that the fibers are not disturbed before spinning. Alternatively, each staple can be picked up and spun separately.

Why prepare the fibers yourself?
Of course, it is possible to purchase fibers that are washed, combed, and ready for spinning, but apart from the fact that this is hardly following the self-sufficiency ethos and is much more expensive than preparing your own fibers, there is a qualitative advantage in starting from the basic fiber. Industrial washing and combing processes stretch and over-clean the fibers, sometimes bleaching them to quite a different color. This is particularly noticeable when you compare them to animal fleeces, which are so different from each other after hand preparation—some curly, some springy and in delicate shades and colors. Bought, prepared slivers all have the same stretched, smooth texture and only a slight color change to tell you which is blond Alpaca and which is wild Black Welsh Mountain sheep.

Hand carding

Carding uses brushes called carders to align the fibers by transfering the wool from one carder to another. It is quite different to combing and produces a "rolag" of wool, which will spin into a fluffy, soft yarn suitable for knitting and weaving into softer clothes that will touch the skin. Combing, by comparison, will spin into a firmer, shinier, and smoother thread, making it more suitable for luster fibers, such as a gentleman's suit.

Carding is more suitable for short fibers, whereas combing is better for longer fibers. Carding is also more suitable for mixing colors and blending textures and colors since you can put different fibers onto the carder.

Carders are bought in pairs and are quite expensive. Unlike combs, they cannot be replaced by other tools. They come in three gauges, for fine, medium, and heavy fibers.

You should mark your carders with "left" and "right" and always use them accordingly. The instructions that follow are for right-handed people; left-handers should interchange right for left, and vice versa.

The carding process

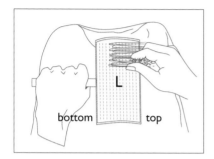

1) Take a small amount of wool and stroke it onto the left carder, starting one-third of the way up from bottom edge. For comfort, rest the left carder on your lap.

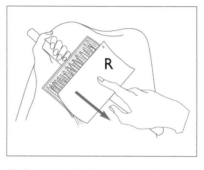

2) Firmly hold the right carder and stroke the fiber on the left carder straight down, pulling clear after the swipe. Keep carding, using light strokes until the threads are parallel and the fibers are aligned and straightened out. The fibers will be on both the right and left carders at this stage.

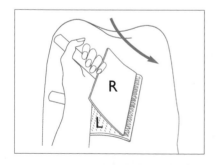

3) Turn the right carder around and transfer the fibers onto the left carder by stroking the right card along the left. This is referred to as "doffing."

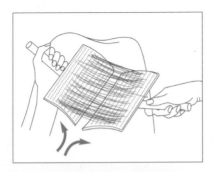 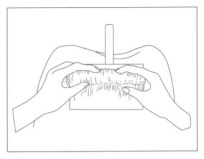

4) Now strip the fibers from the left carder by changing your grip on the right carder and using it to lift the fibers off both of the carders, forming a loose rectangle of carded wool. This is known as a batt of wool.

5) Now transfer the batt to the back of the left carder and roll it up into a sausage either by using your fingers with the right carder. You have made what is called a "rolag," a loosely formed piece of yarn, ready to be stretched and twisted.

Hints and tips
- Control the top, or working, carder by placing the index finger on the back at the base of the handle.
- For even smoother fibers, card again after doffing.
- Start carding from the bottom edge of the carder and work up.
- Stroke the carders. Remember you are drawing out the fiber, not rubbing the carders together. Don't allow the teeth of the carders to touch each other when doffing, or the fibers may embed themselves in the top carder and you may end up folding the fibers over onto each other.
- Remember that one carder is working and one is passive until you "doff off." Always hold the passive carder firmly on your lap for added stability and comfort.

Drum carding

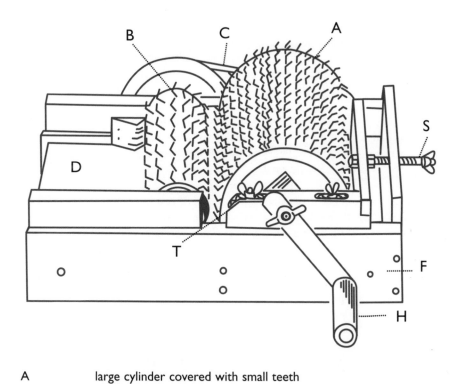

A	large cylinder covered with small teeth
B	small cylinder with large teeth
C	driving belt (this turns the two cylinders in opposite directions)
D	tray on which pieces of teased-out wool are placed to feed them into the smaller cyclinder
F	box or framework
H	handle (this turns the cylinder)
S & T	screws that enable distance between the drums to be adjusted

A drum carder is used instead of hand carders when carding larger quantities of fiber. If used properly, drum carding is three times faster than hand carding. The drum carder consists of a large cylinder and a smaller cylinder covered all round with carding cloth (a rubber or leather sheet covered with small hooked wires) into which fiber is fed and revolved by hand. Clamps fix the carder to the table and the teeth of the smaller drum (the "licker in") and the larger drum are adjusted so that the wool is combed as it passes between them. So by turning the handle and feeding in the wool it will be carded.

The drum carder is useful if you usually spin the same weight of medium fleece into standard yarn or if you like to blend wools. If you find that you like to sample different fibers or use delicate wools for fancy effects, you will probably prefer to hand card.

Drum carders are expensive to buy, so see if you can find a secondhand one. Disliked by the classic spinners as a "barbaric" mistreatment of delicate fibers, it can be a boon to the busy spinner. Once you have obtained and sorted your fleece, you can drum card the lot into large batts ready to spin.

Hints and tips
- Color blending on the drum carder is fun! If you card up two batts of different colors, you can then stack them one on top of the other to feed in again. Alternatively, tear them into strips and feed them in as double- and triple-decker "sandwiches"—giving you a whole range of color mixes to spin up!
- You can do the same with blends of alpaca and wool, or Angora rabbit and wool.
- Only use alpaca, Angora rabbit, or silk on the drum carder with wool to blend; never card them on a drum carder on their own as the carder will stretch and matt the fibers. And never use cashmere on the drum carder, even as a blend, as the teeth are too strong for delicate fibers.
- If you tend to use a variety of fibers, a drum carder may not be a good investment as the gauge of carding cloth cannot be adjusted or changed for different fibers.

Preparing vegetable fibers for spinning

Once you have grown and harvested your own fibers from flax, hemp, or nettle, the stalks need to be rotted by leaving them immersed in water for several days. After this, the next step is to dry them out completely, and then to break or "scutch" them.

Scutching and hackling

The "scutching" process involves breaking up the stalks to release the fibers by hitting them with a heavy wooden item, such as a rolling pin, on a wooden board or table.

As you beat off the woody exterior of the stalks, you end up with a switch of fine, shiny, linen threads, which can then be "hackled": combing out the remaining short tangled threads, which are called "tow," and splitting the flax down into individual fibers. The hackling comb is a fairly inexpensive, but dangerously razor-sharp, piece of equipment that absolutely has to be clamped to the table firmly enough to resist the switch of linen being dragged reluctantly through the teeth.

Preparing cotton

Cotton fiber can only be obtained, prepared, and ready to spin in Europe. The only skill is in making sure that the best Sea Island or Egyptian cotton is purchased, as any of the other varieties have a staple that is too short for a hand spinner to make a good thread. In the United States, "bolls" (the fluffy buds of the cotton shrub) can be bought straight from farmers as a plant. I have found the easiest way to prepare cotton is simply to spin straight from the bolls.

Spinning

With all the preparation behind you, you can now concentrate on the actual spinning of the yarn. The basic principle of spinning fibers by spindle, wheel, or machine is to twist fibers together and stretch them out to form a continuous thread. Wool is the most spinner-friendly fiber to learn on, and it will help you understand the principles of spinning.

Finger spinning

Understanding how a yarn is made is important in knowing how it will behave within a textile, and it is vital for a spinner to gauge the performance of a new fiber. "Finger spinning" is the best way to familiarize yourself with the "twist." The following steps will help you master this simple technique.

1) Place the wool rolag or combed lock in one hand. Take hold of a few threads from the end, by pinching with your thumb and first two fingers of the other hand, and twist them, gently pulling them away from the rolag or lock.

2) Continue twisting and drawing out. The thread will get finer as the hands draw apart and you will have to put more twists in for the amount you stretch. When the fibers are twisted to the correct amount they will become stretchy, like elastic, and you will be able to pull them out into a long length without breaking them. As you twist and stretch the yarn, you will sense a moment when a proper thread is formed. This is the point at which the ratio between how much twist you have put in and how far you draw your hands apart is correct.

3) Once you have pulled out the full length of twisted wool, you will need to wind the thread around something rigid, such as a length of dowelling (see Spindle spinning, page 45).

Spindle spinning

This technique uses a spindle—a stick with a "whorl" (weight) at one end—to easily spin yarn. The wool is attached to the spindle and the spindle is revolved, spinning the wool. The weight of the whorl helps propel the spindle so that when the stick is twirled it will revolve easily. The scope for creativity using a spindle is infinite, as are the size and thickness of the yarn, and it can be used at any time, in any place. A competent spindle spinner can produce a surprisingly large amount of yarn quite quickly once they get into the rhythm.

At first glance, using a simple drop spindle may look slow and complicated, and it might be difficult to see how the yarn will be produced, but with practice, patience, and experience the process will become an enjoyable one. Spindle spinning helps coordinate the hand and eyes and once you have mastered this technique, spinning on the wheel and other more advanced techniques will seem much easier.

Different types of spindle. Inevitably, as spindle spinning evolved in nearly all civilizations, there are dozens of different types of spindle. There are varying lengths and sizes and some have extra features, such as crossed arms to wind the wool round. Heavier spindles will go much faster, but lighter ones are easier to control and are more suitable for finer yarns.

Spindles either have the whorl at the top or at the bottom; those with the weight at the top go much faster, but require a lot of practice to acquire the technique. Ones with the weight at the bottom (see right) are much easier for a beginner to control.

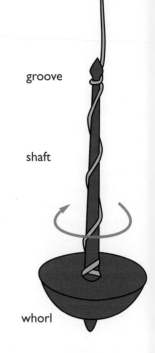

groove

shaft

whorl

Making a drop spindle
To make a working spindle, you only need a length of dowelling sandpapered down and sanded to a blunt point at the top end. Either cut a slanting notch near the top or screw a cup hook in the top. Then insert the other end of the dowelling into a whorl, which can be either a wooden disc, an old CD, or soft clay. Push the whorl towards the bottom of the stick for a bottom-whorl spindle (or towards the top for a faster, top-whorl spindle) and secure. You are now ready to spin!

The principles of drop spindle spinning

The spindle leaves your hands free to work on the yarn, in coordination. The left hand guards the supply of fiber and holds the whole spindle from the top, while the right hand keeps the spindle in motion and draws out the yarn.

1) Attach a piece of starter yarn to the spindle stick by knotting it around the shaft, then winding it around the stick. Finally tie it in a half hitch knot through the groove or pass it through the cup hook at the top of the spindle.

2) Hold the top of the starter yarn and suspend the spindle from it. Practice spinning the spindle clockwise like spinning a top until you can keep it revolving smoothly (or until the starter thread breaks).

3) Pull out a few threads from the end of the rolag or lock with your thumb and first fingers. Hold the threads next to the twisting starter thread and revolve the spindle. As you overlap it by 4–6 in. it will be picked up and twisted in with the revolving thread.

4) Give the spindle another twirl—this means daring to let go of the "new" bit of spun yarn but you will find that the twisting has locked the new fibers into the yarn. Keep going! A good hint is to remember that fibers that have twist in them will not draw out. If you tug at the rolag and it will not draw, it means that you have let some twist into the rolag. Think of your hands as barriers damming the twist into the place you want it.

5) Get into a rhythm and spin until the yarn reaches the floor. At this point you have to unhitch the yarn from the hook or groove and, holding the spindle sideways, roll it on, leaving enough new yarn to thread around the top of the spindle.

6) Once you have filled the spindle, you will have a large cone of yarn sitting on the whorl. This can either be slid off complete or wound off into a ball.

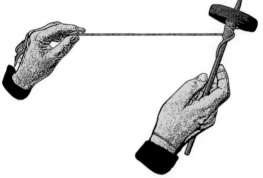

Tips
• To join on another piece of wool, pull out the end of a new rolag and twist this wispy end with the end of the thread on the drop spindle. Then twist the spindle and the new rolag will join on.
• Squash any uneven bits of thread between your fingers, then let the weight of the spindle pull them out.
• If the thread starts to unwind, give the spindle a good twist in a clockwise direction.

"Z" and "S" threads
It is an ancient spinning tradition to refer to threads that have been spun in a clockwise direction as "Z" threads and those spun in a counterclockwise direction as "S" threads. This is because the angle of the twist (or the diagonal line across the thread) matches the direction of the middle line of the letter "Z" or "S" (as illustrated on the right).

It is more usual to spin a thread in a clockwise direction and then ply (see page 49) in a counterclockwise direction.

Plying wool

Plying is a process where two or more spun threads are twisted around each other to create a stronger yarn. It is then known as two-ply, three-ply, four-ply, and so on, after the amount of threads that have been plied together. Single threads can be strong enough to use for weaving and especially for knitting, but plied wool will always be stronger.

The most important rule of plying is that the yarns are twisted around each other in the opposite direction to the direction they were spun in. So a "Z" thread would be plied counterclockwise to make an "S" thread. This creates a rotational equilibrium between the two twists.

To ply the wool, set two or more balls of spun wool in separate bags or bowls (to stop them from rolling around the floor when plying). Tie the two threads together around the shaft of the drop spindle and wrap it around in exactly the same way as for spinning. Holding the two threads instead of the rolag or fibers, twist the spindle counterclockwise. The two threads will instantly ply together and can be wound onto the spindle.

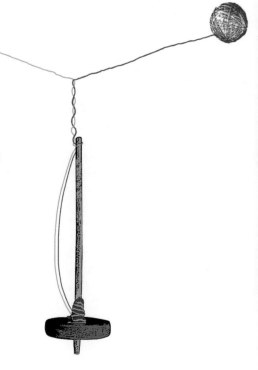

Using a spinning wheel

Once you have mastered, or at least tried, the drop spindle you will find the spinning wheel familiar and in some ways easier to use. If you try to spin on a wheel without trying the spindle first, you are likely to find yourself fuming with frustration!

The mechanism of the spinning wheel is like a spindle on its side; the treadle (operated by the foot) turns the drive band, which rotates the whorl on the spindle. The treadle and wheel are only there to turn the spindle and draw or stretch the thread while the rest of the spinning process, the part the spinner does, is exactly the same as for spindle or finger spinning.

There are various types of spinning wheels, but the two main types are the early spindle wheel and the later bobbin and flyer wheel. The early wheel has just a spindle that turns and twists the yarn; it is then wound onto a spindle by feeding it from the side by hand. The later bobbin wheel uses a bobbin and flyer mechanism to feed the yarn onto the bobbin. It uses foot power to treadle the wheel, which turns the flyer, which then turns the bobbin. This leaves the spinner free to just pull out the fibers and feed them in.

Obtaining a spinning wheel

Spinning wheels are easy to buy. The best advice for a new spinner is to start with the simplest model. There is a flourishing trade in secondhand wheels so it is quite reasonable to think that you could swap a starter wheel later on for a more sophisticated model, although most people become attached to their wheels and simply add to their collection! It is always best to buy through a spinning club or guild, or through one of their publications. If you have woodworking skills, you could even attempt to make your own wheel!

Additionally, there are some simple spinning devices that are suitable for certain projects and tend to be very inexpensive. The famous Charka Indian wheel, beloved of Ghandi, can still be obtained for fine cotton spinning. The "Indian Spinner" is a large flyer and bobbin, wound by hand, and is suitable for making huge sausage thread.

A	wheel	E	treadle
B	drive band	F	footman
C	flyer assembly	G	treadle bar
D	maiden	H	table
		I	distaff

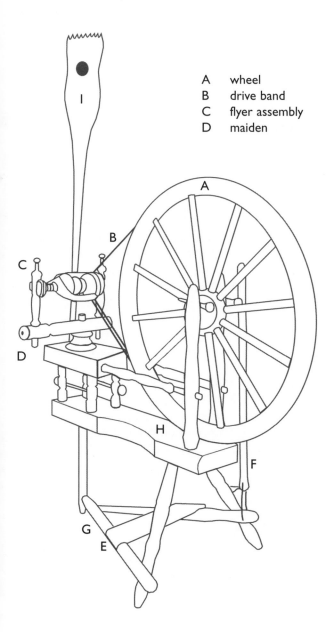

Woolen spinning with wool from carded rolags

1) Make sure your chair has a straight back and that it is at the right height for you to be comfortable.

2) Turn the wheel by flicking the spoke (if you press the rim to turn it, the wheel will eventually develop a wobble).

3) Practice treadling with no yarn attached. Place your foot in the middle of the treadle and watch the axle. Press the treadle down just after the axle has reached the top to make sure it does not reverse. You will notice that, because of its much greater diameter, the wheel's revolutions whiz the flyer round at a great speed, so try treadling at different speeds—aim for a slow rhythmic motion.

4) Attach a starter thread around the bobbin, over the teeth, and out of the orifice at the front.

5) Pull out a few fibers from the rolag and attach them to the starter thread by overlapping them with the rotating starter thread, as with spindle spinning.

6) As the twist flows down the wool and pulls it towards the orifice, allow the right hand fingers to travel a little with it and stretch the end of the rolag. When the yarn is drawn out enough, stroke the fingers back down the fibers towards the left hand. As the new yarn rotates, this will tuck in any stray fibers.

Once you have filled one bobbin, it can be removed and put aside while another bobbin is filled.

Worsted spinning from a combed sliver
Spinning from combed slivers is much like spinning from carded rolags, however the amount you can feed between one hand and the other is shorter because the combed threads are parallel (though this depends on the fiber used). Therefore the movement of the feeding hand is much shorter and quicker than in wool spinning.

Care must be taken not to push back the fibers to prevent the yarn being too thick as this will spoil the alignment of the threads.

Serious worsted spinners will want the fibers evenly spread in the "drafting zone" (the distance between the two hands as they pull out the fibers) to maintain an even amount of wool in each draw.

Plying on the wheel
To ply the wool, you will need to use a bobbin rack to hold the bobbins in place. The traditional rack is called a "Lazy Kate" and it usually comes with the spinning wheel as an accessory.

1) Put a third empty bobbin onto the wheel.

2) Place two or more bobbins on a rack and tie the threads from the bobbins onto a starter thread tied round the bobbin.

3) Turn the wheel in a counterclockwise direction; the single threads will wrap around each other and start to pull onto the bobbin.

This is a much quicker process than spinning as you are simply feeding the threads in and not drawing out. You may feel as though the threads are running away from you onto the bobbin, but beware of holding back and getting too much twist in the ply.

You can fashion your own bobbin rack by pushing two knitting needles through a shoe box horizontally to support the rotating bobbins.

Spinning other fibers

Mohair is spun in locks using the worsted spinning technique. You should hold it quite loosely to allow the shiny fibers to slide past each other. The wheel should be adjusted so that the yarn is pulled in and wound round the bobbin at high speed. The same tension should be used when spinning **cashmere, Angora rabbit,** or other **short luxury fibers**, which should be lightly carded and spun (woolen style) the finer the better.

Serious **linen** spinning requires a whole set of equipment of its own and it can become an addictive pastime. But it is possible to just spin some linen without obtaining the traditional distaff or linen holder and learning to dress and tie it. Linen should be spun "S" direction (i.e., counterclockwise), reflecting the spiral growth of the plant. A switch of linen can be held lightly in the right hand and fed in by the left hand, the fingers wetted in a bowl of water, ensuring a smooth thread. Spin finely and use the thread without plying (after stretching and drying). This will give a strong, smooth weaving yarn that will soften up with washing and handling.

Silk is another fiber that works best drawn out into a fine thread. If you want a thick silk weaving yarn, double or triple it. Four-ply silk cable makes an ideal slightly elastic yarn. I have found that **cotton** works the other way. Even the longest stapled cotton has to be spun with a very short draw and it is best not to try to draw it out too finely. The best handspun cotton thread seems to be a soft, medium thread that can be plied for strength. Think of the sort of yarn you would want for a soft, light shawl rather than the cotton for bed sheets.

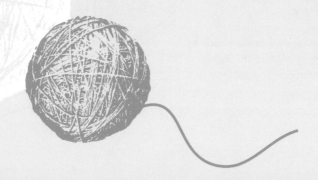

Skeining handspun yarn

Your plied yarn should rest on the bobbin for twenty-four hours if possible; this will set the spin and make it easier to handle. It then has to be wound off into a skein. The traditional tool for doing this is called a "niddy-noddy." By winding the newly spun wool around the niddy-noddy, a skein of even tension will be formed when it is slipped off. You should then tie up the skein in four places before removing it from the niddy-noddy, otherwise you will slip off a heap of tangled threads!

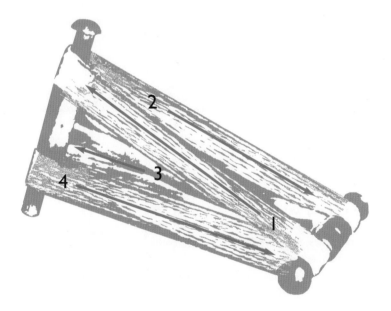

A niddy-noddy is easy to make and cheap to buy, but if you have a bobbin of yarn and no niddy-noddy, you can always wind the yarn off around anything that does not have sharp edges, as at this stage any kinks in the yarn stay forever. You can even wind off around your arm.

Washing the yarn

Washing can make all the difference to your yarn. Fleece straight from the sheep is full of grease and dirt, and even fleece that has been cleaned before spinning will be set and fluffed up by careful washing after it has been spun.

1) Make sure the skeins are securely tied, then prepare a large sink or bowl with hand-hot (104°F) water and lower the skeins in. Press down with flat hands, then lift out and squeeze. This will loosen the dirt and "suint," which is a sort of waterproof sticky coating on the fibers. (Do not use soap at this point—if the wool is washed in soapy water first, the suint will set onto the fibers, making it much more difficult to get it really clean.)

2) Fill the sink with warm water and pure soap flakes or a good-quality detergent. Place the skeins in the suds and pull through the water backwards and forwards, then lift out and squeeze.

3) Rinse with clean water, squeeze, and hang over a clean bar to dry. The yarn can be tensioned with weights but must not be stretched so taut that it will lose its natural elasticity.

For very soft, tender fibers like cashmere and silks, the temperature of the rinsing water should be carefully regulated and

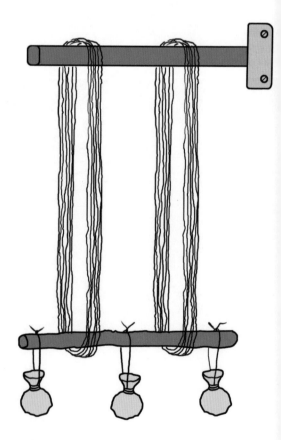

the fibers should not be agitated or moved around too much. The yarn should be left in soapy and then rinsing water for fifteen minutes, and then rolled in a towel and hung to dry. Very fine yarns should be dried flat. If you are allergic to any of the chemicals in fleece, it is best to wear rubber gloves to wash the skeins to prevent any of the chemicals from getting into any cuts you may have on your hands.

Designing your handspun yarn

At this point you have mastered all the skills that will enable you to really start enjoying yourself. Whatever your yarn requirements, you are now in a position to make your own yarns to your specific requirements! Here are a few suggestions for your own exclusively-designed range, but there are hundreds more possibilities. By varying the fibers and mixing plies of two different fibers, changing the thickness of the plies or increasing the number of yarns plied together to three, four, or more, you can create endless designs of yarn.

Super-thick, soft knitting or blanket wool: Use a fleece that is medium length and soft (Southdown). Card enormous fluffy rolags, blending in some colored fleece if you wish. Spin and ply loosely on a drop spindle (the wheel limits the thickness because the threads have to go through the orifice).

Super-fine merino and angora knitting wool: Card rolags of fine merino wool and mix in 10 percent Angora rabbit in the rolags. Spin out as fine as possible, ply with itself, and as the yarn is handled the long hairs will stick out more and more making the yarn more fluffy.

Smooth, shiny tapestry yarn: Comb long, lustrous fleece such as Wenslydale into slivers. Spin into smooth two-ply worsted.

Linen and silk weaving thread: Spin a fine linen thread from combed flax and a fine silk thread and ply the two together.

Fancy twisted wool yarn: Card rolags of soft, medium wool. Divide in half and spin one fine thread and one very thick thread. When the two are plied together the resulting yarn will be thick and thin like a twisted barley sugar.

Dyeing

Using natural dyestuffs that can be grown or gathered is the most self-sufficient way to color textiles. It is also more environmentally responsible, avoiding the use of the many petrochemicals and heavy metals necessary to make synthetic colors. Natural dyestuffs are made from the leaves, roots, and stems of plants, shrubs, and trees, and this chapter looks at the most easily obtainable sources of permanent color and the recipes that will give the best results.

A historical overview

The oldest known dyed fabrics are from the Indus Valley. They were dyed using indigo and date back to between 2500 and 1500 BC. Around 1600 BC fabric dyed with murex seashell was unearthed in Crete. Egyptian dyers were recorded as using madder and safflower to dye fabrics in the first century AD.

The great guilds of medieval European dyers perfected the use of local and imported dyestuffs to make brilliant colors for the clothing of courtiers and to weave the huge tapestries still glowing in our museums today. Color sources used included plants, trees, insects, and seashells, and recipes were closely guarded secrets.

In 1864 the first synthetic dye was created by a young British chemist named William Perkin. By the late 1800s most of the industrially-produced cloth in the world was synthetically dyed, and the skills—along with most of the recipes for making natural color—were lost and forgotten. Several attempts have been made to revive the use of plant colors since, with only moderate success, as they have proved difficult to recreate without access to the tried-and-tested methods of bygone centuries.

Grow your own color

A surprisingly diverse range of colors can be created using garden plants, hedgerow weeds, and a few other simple ingredients. Though very little energy is needed to make these colors, they do take time to develop and patience to prepare. Most plants used for dyeing have unremarkable yellow or white flowers, bearing no relationship whatsoever to the colors they will give.

Space
A dye plot can be as large or as small as you choose. The amount of color yield varies from species to species and is dependent on various factors, such as the amount of sunshine and the time of year. A 21.5 square foot bed of dyeplants should give a knitter or spinner enough color for the year. Some

plants that are very useful to the dyer are technically weeds. These include nettles, dandelion, weld (which loves the cracks in concrete), and woad, which once established will pop up all over the place! Seeds or small plants can be obtained from craft suppliers, but the best source is from other dyers through guilds and clubs. The plants should, if possible, be in raised beds for good drainage.

Which plants are best to grow?

Everyone will have their own favorite dyeplants and, of course, the planting can change from one year to the next. Woad, madder, Ladies Bedstraw, weld, goldenrod, Dyer's Greenwood, marigold, coreopsis, buckthorn, iris, camomile, safflower, and dahlia are plants that give dyes that are colorfast as well as reliable and easy to use. Alkanet, apple twigs, gorse, heather, rhubarb, tansy, nettles, dandelions, and feverfew will all give beautiful colors and nobody knows what other color secrets are hidden in your garden or even in your window box!

Natural dyes without a garden

Not all of us have enough space for a dye garden or even to grow some plants to sample, but we can all recycle plant matter to use as dyes. Avocado pear skins will give a range of pinks (depending on the variety and the time of year). Beetroot, onion skins, carrot tops, carrot parings, swede skins, and tired spinach leaves will all have some effect with the use of mordants. Then there are weeds, of which nettle, ragwort, and dandelion are definitely not endangered so can be picked from the side of the road and will give delicate colors.

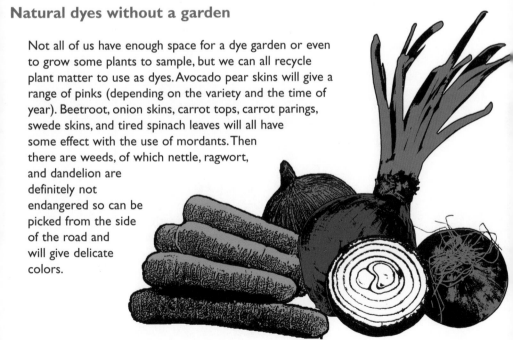

Buying natural dyes

There are some famous historic dyes that once were extremely valuable and traded around the world, such as the prized saffron (which is worth more than gold, weight for weight), Persian madder root, and blocks of pure indigo. Generally, however, natural dye plants are not expensive to buy. The more common dyestuffs can be bought from a local craft shop or postal supplier for reasonable amounts. Many dye plants are still farmed in parts of Turkey and Armenia for distribution to specialist textile makers and dye merchants around the world.

Harvesting and storing dye plants

Picking and storing your plants correctly can greatly improve color quality and yield. As most of the traditions and expertize in handling dye plants has been forgotten, trial and error are the best guides.

Like edible herbs, dye plants should be gathered early in the morning on a fine day. Root dyes like madder should be dug when the earth is damp. Long, woody-stemmed plants like weld should be loosely tied and hung upside down in a draughty, dry room. If you are collecting seeds or if small bits are prone to fall off, as with goldenrod, hang upside down inside a paper bag. Flower heads or short-stemmed plants should be dried on a wire rack to allow air to circulate. I have tried drying plants in the oven on the lowest heat on paper towels but the results weren't as good; microwaves definitely don't work!

Store the dried plant material in brown paper bags. Plastic bags and plastic food containers seem to soften the plants but don't worry if they crumble— the important thing is that they are stored correctly, in dry conditions. Hard stalks, roots, and seeds are best stored whole in paper bags and ground when needed.

The dyeing process

Fabrics are dyed by a long process of extracting the color and then soaking and simmering the fabric with the dye. Most plant dyes also require the use of something called a "mordant," which improves the take-up of the dyestuff. The individual methods of dyeing with different dye plants will be detailed on pages 72–83, but here are the basic principles:

Extracting dye from plants
The process of extracting dye from plants varies from plant to plant. Roots, berries, leaves, and flower heads require slightly different methods but in general the plant stuff is first macerated, chopped, or ground up. It is then boiled or simmered. Most plant material needs very little heat; only a few need to be boiled to extract the dye. On the whole, the longer and lower the simmer, and as little water as possible (just enough to cover the chopped plant stuff), the better. Sometimes the material is then fermented, as with woad.

Making a decoction
A decoction is the resulting liquor after plant matter has been boiled. In general, I find this the best way to prepare small to medium amounts of dye as you can bottle up the dye liquid and keep it until needed. In cool conditions, dye can keep for up to a year.

To make a decoction, the chopped and boiled plant material should be steeped in the water it was boiled in for up to twenty-four hours. The plants are then strained off and discarded, leaving a clear, deeply-colored dye liquid. The strength of this decoction will depend on the proportion of plant material used to water, though water can be added to dilute the strength of the mixture. For simplicity's sake, it is a good idea to make the dye with 7 oz. of dye plant to every 4¼ cups of water; this way you know that every 4¼ cups will have 7 oz. of dye plant.

Alternative methods for dyeing are to place the plant material in a muslin bag and cook it with the textile to be dyed. For really large amounts, cook the plant, take it out of the liquid, and then cook the textile in the liquid.

Preparing the fabric
All wool and animal fibers should be thoroughly washed before dyeing. Soak your carefully tied skeins of yarn or fabric pieces in tepid water for a minimum of thirty minutes. Cook cottons and linens in a spoonful of washing soda by bringing them to a boil, then turning off the heat and leaving them to soak for up to twenty-four hours. Remove the materials from the soak and squeeze them out evenly before dyeing. If you are not going to dye all of the yarn, this is a good point at which to thoroughly dry and store it.

Mordanting
Most plant dyes require a mordant to fix the dye permanently onto the fibers. Mordanting can be done in a number of ways, but the easiest process is to dissolve the mordant in water, then to add to a mordant bath in which the fabric is heated and soaked. Individual recipes for mordants are given on pages 68–71. Mordanting and dyeing *can* be done in one step in a mixture of mordant and dyestuff, but I have found that the resulting dye is not so light-fast, so it is best to do the mordanting and dyeing in two separate steps. This also means that a large amount of material can be mordanted in one go and kept aside for different dyes.

Mordants come from an enormous number of seemingly random sources but they have all been found to improve take-up of the dyestuff and to fix the dye permanently onto the fibers. Most mordants come from naturally occurring mineral deposits, such as alum and copper. Alkaline mordants include urine and wood ash. Citric fruits, rhubarb, and sumac leaves are all acidic mordants. Mordanting chemicals can also be found in some familiar household substances like vinegar, washing soda, and copper coins.

Equipment for mordanting and dyeing

Very little equipment is needed for mordanting and dyeing. You will need a liquid thermometer, as monitoring the temperature—keeping it low but not too low—is vital for best results. The other must-have is large pans—textiles need space when they are dyeing. Think of the yarn or fabric as a goldfish that needs space to swim.

Dye buckets can be just that: old metal buckets. There is a great deal of concern about the metal content of the dye pot affecting the color but it will do so only slightly, so there is no need to buy an expensive stainless steel dye bath (although they are easier to handle and clean out). Large, old pans from a garage sale or cheap catering equipment shop will do. Copper, iron, and aluminum pots will all modify the colors slightly. The greatest treasure is an old tea urn, which is ideal for use as an indigo dye bath since the temperature can be maintained and the urn, being made of stainless steel, will be easy to clean of indigo scum between dyeings. However, if you don't have one, a large, old pan will do just as well.

You will also need scales that weigh up to 2 lbs. 3 oz., along with stirring rods, wooden spoons, or sticks; beware of stirrers with rough edges if you are dyeing delicate fabrics or yarns. Metal barbecue tongs or wooden laundry tongs are invaluable. Finally, you will need a place to hang your dyed materials—an outside washing line is ideal but a drying rack over a plastic bowl will do fine.

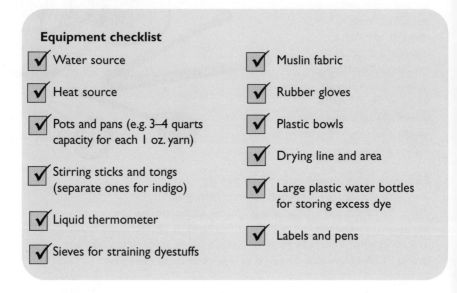

Equipment checklist

☑ Water source

☑ Heat source

☑ Pots and pans (e.g. 3–4 quarts capacity for each 1 oz. yarn)

☑ Stirring sticks and tongs (separate ones for indigo)

☑ Liquid thermometer

☑ Sieves for straining dyestuffs

☑ Muslin fabric

☑ Rubber gloves

☑ Plastic bowls

☑ Drying line and area

☑ Large plastic water bottles for storing excess dye

☑ Labels and pens

Energy efficiency

The self-sufficient dyer can make the most of the least amount of heat for the lengthy processes involved in successful natural dyeing. "Haybox" and "retained heat cooking" are age-old methods that can be used to conserve energy. They are perfect for the long cooking processes that give the best dye results. In fact, many natural dyes need almost no heat, and many don't work well in temperatures above 104°F–122°F. In conventional cooking, once the pot has reached the required temperature, it only remains on the heat to retain that temperature. With dyeing, if a pot is heated and then put into an insulated box, most of the heat is prevented from escaping and the dyeing process continues indefinitely. Any kind of insulated container will do, as long as it can withstand heat. A stout cardboard box with a wooden board or wire rack placed in it on which the pot should stand is fine. The insulating material can be hay, straw, wool, feathers, or cushions, and should fit snugly between the pot and the sides of the box. The cooking container should have a tight-fitting lid so as not to lose moisture and heat. The best use of haybox cooking is to maintain long, steady heat once the initial temperature has been reached.

The grandchild of the haybox is the "solar box." This is just like the haybox except that it is a wooden box with a glass lid that should be positioned where it will catch the warmth of the sun. Even in relatively gloomy conditions you can get a good color in four or five days. Another method of energy efficient dyeing is simpler solar dyeing, which works very well for the home dyer for small quantities of yarn or fabric. Just place a jam jar with some dye and a small quantity of mordanted yarn in it on the window sill; the energy from sunlight will give a good color in four to five days.

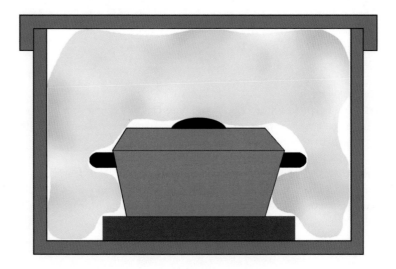

Recipes for mordants

Here are details for how to prepare and use various mordants. None of the following ingredients are either harmful, poisonous, or environmentally hazardous. In some cases the recipes include an "assistant," used to improve the performance of the mordant or to alter the shade.

Alum
Alum rock is prized because it is an effective mordant that gives true colors. Whereas many of the other mordants add a greenish or yellowish tinge to the dye color, alum gives clear, bright shades with no underlying hue. Available from chemists or craft shops.

Quantities: use 10 percent alum to weight of all fabrics, plus 5 percent cream of tartar for wool, silk, and all protein fibers only. Cream of tartar is not suitable for linen and cotton.
Method: damp the skeins or fabric with water. To make the bath, fill a large pan with water and heat to 176°F. Dissolve the alum and cream of tartar in boiling water and add to the mordant bath, stirring vigorously to dissolve all the granules. Put the dampened skeins into the alum mordant and simmer at 158°F for 40 minutes. Turn down the heat to 86°F and continue simmering for one hour. Remove the pan from the heat and soak for two hours. After mordanting, do not rinse the material; either dye it immediately or hang it up to dry and store in a paper bag.

Copper sulphate
Used since Egyptian times, copper sulphate can be bought as a blue powder and used to "green" a yellow dye, and to give fine greens and very bright blues as an afterbath to indigo.

Quantities: use 15 percent copper sulphate to weight of fabric.
Method: to make the bath, fill a large pan with hot tap water. Dissolve the copper sulphate in a little hot water and add it to the mordant bath. Add

2 tablespoons of acetic acid (white vinegar) and
stir well. Put the yarn or fabric into the copper
mordant and heat to 176°F. Cook for 1 to
1½ hours for a medium-thick fabric, then remove from the heat and
soak in the mordant for up to, but no longer than, one hour. Thoroughly rinse
the yarn or fabric.

Another recipe for making copper mordant is to place a copper bracelet in a
jam jar with 4 teaspoons of acetic acid (white vinegar) and add enough warm
water to cover the bracelet. Leave it to stand for four days, shaking occasionally. The water will turn bluish. Make the dye bath up as for copper sulphate.

Wood ash
Use the whitest wood ash you can
get. If you use birch on your
barbecue, hold on to the white ash.

Quantities: use 50 percent wood
ash to weight of material and 2
cups of water.
Method: put the ash in a jam jar
and pour enough warm water to
fill the jam jar. Give it a good
shake and leave it to stand for one
week. The liquid should become crystal
clear and extremely alkaline. To make the
bath, fill a large pan with water and heat to 176°F. Strain the liquid from the
jam jar and pour it into the mordant bath. Add the material to the bath and
simmer at 104°F–122°F for a minimum of one hour. Remove from the heat
and leave to soak overnight (but no longer), then rinse and dry. This can give
wonderful results, but the amount made is rather trial and error and it
requires a lot of good ash—and time.

Iron
Ferrous sulphate, known as "copperas," has been used in dyeing for centuries. As a mordant it "saddens" (makes grayer) and darkens colors, and was traditionally used to make blacks and dark tones, usually by adding it to the dye bath as an after-mordant.

Quantities: use 6^1/$_3$ cups of mordant per 7 oz. fabric.
Method: soak about 20 iron nails, or, best of all, a horse's shoe, in mild white vinegar water for a week (four parts water to one part vinegar). This will make about 12^1/$_2$ cups of iron mordant. Leave to settle, then strain the resulting rusty liquor before use. To make the bath, fill a large pan with water, add the strained liquid, and put the dampened material into the iron mordant. Simmer at 140°F–158°F for 45 minutes, then remove the material from the mordant, rinse, and dry.

Gallnuts
Gallnuts, galls, or oak apples are the home of the gall wasp and are found on oak trees. They contain 50–70 percent tannin and have been used throughout the world for dyeing and leather tanning. Black ink is made from gallnuts.

Quantities: use 20 percent weight of gallnuts to weight of material.
Method: there are two ways of preparing the rock-hard gallnuts. Firstly, you can grind them to a powder with a blender or hammer and grind them in a mortar and pestle. Then soak and cook the powder by adding enough water to comfortably cover the powder and allow for evaporation. Simmer for 30 minutes, then strain. Alternatively, you can soak the gallnuts overnight, then boil for 1^1/$_2$ hours and strain into the mordant bath. (Cotton should always be "galled" or simmered with tannin for 45 minutes, even if another mordant is used in addition.) To make the bath, fill a large pan with water and heat to

104°F. Add the strained gallnut liquor. Put in the material and raise the temperature to 176°F. Cook for one hour, turn off the heat, and leave to soak for 3 to 4 hours.

Plant mordants
The best plant and vegetal mordants are:
- rhubarb stalks—give a yellowish hue;
- rhubarb leaves—give a very pale green, but these are poisonous so be careful;
- privet leaves—give a greenish hue;
- sumac leaves—give no color;
- nettles—give a brownish green hue;
- lemon skins—give no color.

For plant mordants, pour boiling water over the plant stalks/leaves/skins. A rough guide is to use 25 percent plant matter to weight of fabric. Simmer for one hour and strain. Pour the liquid into a large pan filled with water and heated to 176°F and add the material. Simmer for a minimum of 45 minutes, remove from the heat, then leave to soak for up to but no longer than 24 hours.

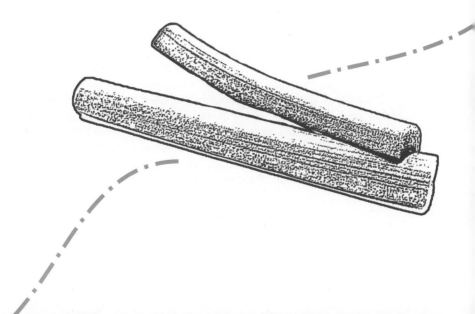

Recipes for dye plants

The following recipes will explain how to grow or
obtain, prepare, and use each plant. For ease of use, the
plants have been grouped by the colors they give.

Red and pink

Madder (Rubia tinctoria)
There are many species of madder plant but none of them produces as
much color as *Rubia tinctoria*. It grows in Europe, the Americas, and Asia
(particularly Turkey) but can also be grown in England and even Scotland,
where it was known as "Maud." The dye is contained in the roots, beneath
the woody root bark. Because it is difficult to grow from seed, try to get
hold of small plants from friends. Once established, madder will sprawl all
over the place and is best confined to raised beds or planters, where it has
to be grown for two years before being uprooted for dye. If the plants are
exposed to sun and rich soil, the dye roots are as thick as pencils and a
dozen plants will give roughly 6 lbs. 10 oz. of roots (remember to save a few
to replant). Harvest with a digging fork and carefully wash off the earth.

At this point opinion divides: Some advise soaking the roots in water for
several days and then grinding them to a paste with washing soda. The other
option is to dry the roots in a warm place for 4 or 5 days, then grind them
into a powder. Make a decoction with the ground root paste or powder,
making the strength 7 oz. of madder per 4$\frac{1}{4}$ cups of water.

Quantities: use 25 percent weight of madder to weight of material.
Method: madder can be mordanted with alum to give geranium red or
mordanted with copper to give a brownish pink. Follow either the alum and
copper mordanting recipes on pages 68–9, but don't allow the temperature to
exceed 140°F or a brownish color will be released that will spoil the bright
red and copper colors. Pour the right amount of madder dye decoction into a

large pan or dye bath. You will need 4¼ quarts of water for every 3½ oz. of material. Heat for 30 minutes, slowly bringing up the temperature of the dye bath until 140°F has been reached. Then hold at this temperature for a minimum of one hour, stirring occasionally. Remove from the heat and leave the skeins or fabric to cool in the dye bath. If you want orange shades, add one teaspoon of lemon juice to the dye bath for every 3½ oz. of material as an afterbath. For pinkish shades, add one teaspoon of washing soda per 3½ oz. of material. Remove the skeins or fabric from the dye bath and rinse in clear water, then hang up to dry.

Lady's Bedstraw (Galium verum) and goosegrass (Galium aparine), also known as cleavers
These low scrambling plants with fragrant flowers are lesser madder plants, native to northern and western Europe. The root systems are much smaller than madder roots and, although Lady's Bedstraw will give a pleasant light pink, it is hardly enough to dig it up for. Goosegrass (which has the same sticky leaves as the true madder and is known as the scourge of gardens), on the other hand, is such a nuisance that it is dug up anyway, and in large enough quantities is worth saving for dyeing.

Quantities: use 120 percent weight of Lady's bedstraw and 200 percent weight of goosegrass to weight of material.
Method: as for madder.

Safflower (Carthamus tinctoria)
Safflower is known as dyer's thistle and gives pink and red dyes on silk and cotton. (It also gives yellow dyes on wool, see page 82.) It is an annual plant and grows to 3 ft. 3 in. with brilliant orange and red flower heads. Because it is susceptible to frosts, the seeds should be sprouted indoors and planted out after the frosts. It likes a sunny position and poor soil, and the flowers can be picked and its petals removed and dried as they bloom, from mid-summer onwards.

Quantities: use 200 percent weight of safflower petals to weight of fabric.

Method: soak the loose petals for one hour, then tie them in a muslin bag and put under running water for a few minutes. Soak in the muslin bag in fresh water for another hour, then take the petals out of the muslin bag and put them into a glass or ceramic bowl large enough to contain the cotton or silk to be dyed. Add enough cold water to cover the petals and the material, but don't add the material yet. Gradually add enough washing soda so that the liquid measures pH 11. Allow to stand for one hour; the liquid will turn red. Then strain the liquid into a separate bowl and discard the petals. Add enough white vinegar or lemon juice to the liquid to make the solution pH 6. Now add the unmordanted material and soak overnight. In the morning the material should be bright pink. Remove from the dye, rinse in running water, then hang up to dry.

Brazilwood
The sawdust from the brazilwood tree, *Caesalpinia echinata*, is a cheap and sustainable dyestuff that has been used in Europe since ancient times. It yields a surprising amount of bright, crimson dye that, with different mordants, will give a profusion of reds and magentas.

Quantities: for reds, use 25 percent brazilwood chips and dust to weight of material.
Method: put the chips/dust in a muslin bag and soak overnight in a bowl with just enough water to cover the chips. Simmer for one hour in the same water, then strain the dye into the dye bath. Put in the mordanted material and simmer at 158°F–176°F for 45 minutes. Remove from the heat and leave the material to soak in the dye bath overnight. Rinse out in cold water. For magentas, add 1 1/3 oz. of washing soda per 3 1/2 oz. of material after simmering. Remove from the heat and leave the material to soak in the dye bath overnight. Rinse out in cold water.

Blue

Woad (Isatis tinctoria)
Historically, woad is one of the most widely used dye plants. It contains the chemical indican that gives a strong blue dye. This is the same dye as found in the indigo plant *(Indigofera tinctoria)*, which contains a lot more indican than woad but is difficult to grow in cold climates. Woad is cold hardy and is the easiest of the forty or so plants containing indigo to grow in the garden. In the first year of growth a rosette of large dark leaves is formed and this is the source of the blue dye. In the early summer of the second year the plant grows a long stem that produces lots of small, yellow flowers and then black seeds (which can give other colors). The big tap root absorbs lots of nutrients and in some cases four crops of leaves per year can be harvested. The leaves boast antiseptic properties and have been used for centuries to cure ulcers.

The most complicated methods and recipes for natural dyes are for the plants that contain indigo. The indican chemical within the plants will only enter into the fibers in a completely oxygen-free environment, so the dye bath must not be stirred, there must be no splashing, and the surface should be disturbed as little as possible. Only under these circumstances will the indicant enter the fibers. Note that at this stage the yarn and dye bath are not actually blue. The dye bath is a sort of petrol/yellow/dark liquid and the yarn looks yellowish/green. It is only when the wool is (carefully) removed from the dye bath that it starts to oxygenate and turn blue. The blue will penetrate fully as the wool is successively dipped in the dye bath and oxygenated several times, so dipping and airing are a feature of most indigo dyes.

Quantities: use 50 percent weight of leaves to weight of yarn for a light shade; use up to 400 percent for the deepest shades.
Method: tear the leaves into small pieces and put them in a plastic bucket. Pour boiling water to cover the leaves completely and leave to steep for 30 minutes. Squeeze the leaves for maximum juice before discarding them, then strain the sherry-colored liquid into a separate bucket. Add 4 teaspoons of

washing soda or 2 teaspoons of ammonia (or urine) to the strained liquid (or double these quantities for deeper shades); it should turn dark green. Aerate the mixture by whisking vigorously or pouring from one bucket to another, until the froth turns blue or blue/green. Heat the liquid to 122°F and slowly and carefully sprinkle one teaspoon of sodium dithionite, thiourea dioxide (which can be purchased as Spectralite), or any reducing agent per 3¹/₂ oz. material; this will remove the oxygen from the dye. Take care when using the reducing agent, as the chemicals may cause irritation. After this has been added, do not stir or disturb the surface. Remove from the heat and leave the liquid to stand for 15 minutes. Gently add the wetted (unmordanted) wool skeins without disturbing the surface and leave to stand for 10 minutes. Then carefully remove the material without letting it drop back into the dye bath; you can do this by quickly lifting it out and over a plastic bowl. Wave the skeins vigorously to aerate them, then dip back in the dye bath and air alternately, until dark enough. Now fill a sink with cold water and add 2 tablespoons of white vinegar. Immerse the skeins in the vinegar water to preserve the color and finish by washing with warm, mildly soapy water to remove excess dye.

Dried woad leaves
If you dry or freeze whole or chopped woad it loses its "blue powers."
However, the dried leaves were traditionally made into balls and stored as
such, and this process, somehow, preserved the indican. If you want to try
your hand at making woad balls, follow these instructions, though the process
is a difficult one and the blue can easily be lost. Alternatively, it is now possible
to buy powdered woad.

Quantities: as for fresh woad leaves.
Method: blend the leaves in a food processor and allow the chopped leaves
to macerate in their juices for 30 minutes to soften. Roll the minced leaves
into balls slightly larger than tennis balls, and dry in a warm place for 4 to 6
weeks until they are wood-hard. When they are needed, the balls can be
mashed down with a little tepid water, then placed in a dye bath and boiling
water poured over. When the liquid turns a sherry color, sprinkle two
teaspoons of ammonia or washing soda per ball and continue the process as
for fresh woad.

Powdered indigo
Powdered indigo comes from the Asian shrub, *Indigoferens tinctoria*. You will
have to buy the strongest indigo either as a powder or as a block. Many
recipes have evolved over the centuries, reflecting the various cultures that
have used it. This recipe is the simplest and gives great results. Use on
unmordanted wool.

Quantities: 15 percent weight powdered indigo to weight of material.
Method: dissolve 1 oz. washing soda in 1 fl. oz. boiling water per 3½ oz. of
material, then allow to cool slightly. In a glass jug, mix ½ oz. indigo powder for
every 3½ oz. of material to a paste with 2 teaspoons of the warm water.
Gradually add the washing soda solution to the indigo paste and stir well
before adding a further 4 teaspoons warm water until the paste has dissolved.
Put 12½ cups of water into a dye bath and heat to 122°F. Very gently add the
indigo solution to the bath by lowering in the jar with the solution and tipping
the liquid out under the surface, taking care not to disturb the surface of the

dye bath. Sprinkle 1 oz. sodium dithionite, thiourea dioxide (which can be purchased as Spectralite), or any reducing agent per 7 oz. of unmordanted material for light to medium colors, or per 3½ oz. of material for deep colors, over the surface of the liquid. Leave for 30–60 minutes, keeping the temperature constant. The dye bath can be concentrated by adding 4 teaspoons of ammonia or aged urine. Continue the process as for fresh woad.

Yellow and orange

Weld (Reseda luteola)
Known as "Wild Mignonette" or "Dyer's Rocket," weld has a long history of use as a dye. It was used to dye wedding clothes and the robes of vestal virgins in first century Rome, perhaps because of the clarity and purity of the color. By medieval times, when it was a comparatively cheap dye, it was used to dye yellow hats that denoted Jews in Venice and later in Elizabethan England, and Christians in medieval Persia. Mixed with woad or indigo it dyed that most famous of colors, Lincoln green, as worn by Robin Hood. A hardy biannual, it is best grown from seed started indoors in mid winter and planted out after the frosts. Six or seven rosettes, or two whole plants, will dye about 1 lb. of yarn or fabric a bright, fast color. The whole plant can be dried and chopped, although the big hollow stems of the late summer do not give much color, and in this state it can be kept indefinitely. Weld gives a range of yellows, depending on which mordant has been used before dyeing. Alum mordant will give brilliant primrose yellow and copper mordant will give green/yellow hues.

Quantities: use 50–60 percent weight of weld to weight of material.
Method: whichever mordant you use, the dyeing process will be the same.
Weld needs to be cooked twice to extract the maximum amount of color
from the plant. Steep 1³/₄ oz. of weld for every 3¹/₂ oz. of material for 30
minutes in 8¹/₂ cups cold water per 3¹/₂ oz. material, then boil in a dyepan for
30 minutes with one-half teaspoon of salt. Strain off the liquor into a
container large enough to store it; reserve both the liquor and the boiled
weld. Repeat the process using the boiled weld and the same amount of fresh
cold water, but without the salt. Strain off the liquor. In a large pan mix the
two liquors together for a stronger dye, then put the mordanted wool skeins
or fabric into the dye bath. Add enough water to top up the dyebath to 4¹/₄
quarts for every 3¹/₂ oz. of material and simmer at 140°F–158°F for one hour,
stirring occasionally, then leave to cool in the soup. To brighten the color on
wool, add one teaspoon of household ammonia or stale urine, and leave to
soak for 10 minutes. Remove the wool or fabric from the dye bath and rinse
until clear. Dry thoroughly.

Dyer's Greenwood (Genista tinctoria)
This short shrub has spikes of yellow flowers and later pea-like pods. The
flowers and tender twigs and leaves at the end of the branches are used for
dyeing; it takes two years before the shrub has enough for it to be used.
The shrubs were originally from Anjou and Dyer's Greenwood still grows in
abundance in the dry soil there. A late dye plant, it can be used until the
mid autumn. The dried or fresh flower heads and green twigs give a cool
yellow color very much in demand for centuries. When used with woad it
makes Kendal green.

Quantities: use 60 percent Dyer's Greenwood to weight of material (the
longer the soak in the dye bath the fewer dye plants are needed).
Method: As with weld, the twigs and leaves need to be double cooked to
extract the maximum amount of color. Steep 2 oz. of the plant for
30 minutes in 2 quarts cold water per 3¹/₂ oz. material, then boil in a dyepan for
30 minutes with a dash of white vinegar. Strain off the liquor into a container
large enough to store it; reserve both the liquor and the boiled

Dyer's Greenwood. Repeat the process using the boiled plant and the same amount of fresh cold water. Strain off the liquor and place into a large dye bath with the mordanted wool, topping up the liquid to make 4 ¼ quarts per every 3½ oz. wool or fabric. Simmer at 140°F–158°F for 15 minutes and leave to cool in the soup. Remove the wool from the dye bath and rinse. Alum and cream of tartar mordant gives clear yellow after 15 minutes of simmering; longer simmering and steeping gives gold.

Goldenrod (Solidago canadensis, or Vergaurea in Europe)
A perennial plant that is very easy to grow. There are many species of goldenrod, all of which produce a permanent mustard yellow of various strengths. Plants grow up to 4 ft. and are often used by florists to make bouquets. The whole plant can be dried and chopped but the best color is obtained from fresh flower heads. They were and still are used as herbal remedies for kidney problems and were a traditional dyestuff in northern Europe and Scandinavia. It was particularly used for dyeing calico. Pick in full flower and use the flowering tops only. It gives a golden/maize yellow on material that has been mordanted with alum. Rhubarb mordant gives gold colors.

Quantities: use 60 percent goldenrod to weight of material (the longer the soak in the dye bath, the fewer dye plants are needed).
Method: cook the flowering tops for 30 minutes in water, then strain off the colored liquor. Put this liquor and mordanted wool into the dye bath and simmer at 140°F–158°F for one hour, then leave to cool in the dye bath.

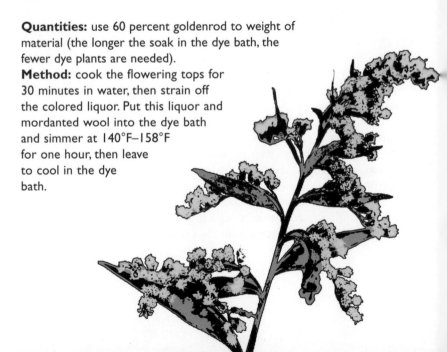

Golden yellow

Dyer's Buckthorn (Rhamnus tinctoria)
There are, confusingly, around
100 varieties of Buckthorn (*Rhamnus*)
but this one has been historically
famous as a source of orange, yellows, and greens. It is a shrub so it needs at
least two seasons before the leaves and twigs are harvested for dyeing.

Quantities: use 20 percent berries to weight of wool.
Method: berries should be dried and ground to a powder or soaked and
boiled. Strain the berry soup and add it to the dye bath. Cook for 30 minutes
to 1 hour until color develops, then put the mordanted wool in at 176°F and
turn off the heat. Leave the wool to soak for 24 hours, stirring occasionally
for complete fastness. It gives primary yellow with an alum mordant or egg-
yolk yellow with tannic mordants. Alum and copper mordant can give brilliant
sap green.

Marigold (Calendula officinalis)
Sown early spring to early summer, this old English marigold has bright orange
flowers, which are edible and can be used in salads or rice dishes, or to make
ointments for wounds. The flowers are one of the rare cases of a dye plant
that actually looks like the color it dyes. The fresh flower heads will give
brilliant orange and orange/yellows. If processed carefully, the dried flowers
will give a slightly dimmer orange.

Quantities: use 200 percent flowers to weight of wool.
Method: flower heads should be picked in full bloom and in full sunshine,
then steeped for no more than one hour (or they will break down). Next
simmer for one hour maximum at 104°F until the color develops. Strain the
liquid from the simmered heads and add the mordanted wool, simmer at
158°F until the color develops, then remove from the heat, take out the
material, and rinse immediately—steeping at this stage dulls the color.
Marigolds give orange/yellow with an alum or cream of tartar mordant, and
greens with a copper mordant.

Saffron
If you want to try an ancient dyestuff, saffron is simple but very expensive to use.

Quantities: use 40 percent weight saffron to weight of wool.
Method: Boil saffron in 3 quarts of water per 1 oz. of wool or silk for 30 minutes. Strain the resulting liquid into a dye bath. Immerse mordanted material (an alum mordant is best) and simmer at 140°F for 30 minutes. Rinse in cold water.

Safflower (Carthamus tinctoria)
As well as giving pink and red dyes on silk and cotton (see page 73), safflower will give yellow dyes on wool.

Quantities: use 100 percent weight of safflower petals to weight of fabric.
Method: soak the loose petals for one hour. The water will turn a bright yellow. Simmer unmordanted wool in this liquid at around 104°F–122°F for 45 minutes. Remove the wool from the dye, rinse in running water, then hang up to dry.

Coreopsis (Coreopsis tinctoria)
A familiar hardy perennial that flowers from early summer to early autumn. Coreopsis will dye best on wool and silk and, with the right mordants, gives stunning reds and oranges. Gives bright yellow with an alum mordant, and reds with an iron and washing soda mordant.

Quantities: as for marigold.
Method: as for marigold.

Black

Iris (Iris pseudocorous)
True black is the most difficult color to achieve for the natural dyer, but the roots of the common yellow flag iris will give a fine black. They like to grow in damp places but will make a large amount of root each year. Be aware that the roots are poisonous; however, they are also very unappetizing so it is unlikely that they will be ingested in large quantities by mistake.

Quantities: use 100 percent weight root to weight of wool.
Method: dry the roots for one week, then chop them and simmer for one hour. Next, pour the soup into the dye bath and add the yarn mordanted in iron. Dye the material for a minimum of one hour. A strong black will develop slowly.

Other colors

Some tried and tested dye plants from the garden and hedgerow follow. With all these plants, the quantities, times, and methods are the same as for marigold (see page 81).

Garden plants
- camomile—gives a yellow/green but can be more effective as a mordant
- tansy—gives yellow, gold, or olive green with alum
- dahlia—gives yellow to orange with alum
- feverfew—gives a light yellow-green with chrome
- yarrow—gives yellow with alum
- betony—gives dark yellow
- lavender—gives a pale pink with lemon juice and alum
- sunflower seeds—gives blue with copper

Weeds and hedgerow plants
- agrimony—gives gold, brassy yellow, and orange on wool
- blackberry—gives pinks with alum and white vinegar
- horse chestnuts—soak in water for shades of brown
- dandelion flowers—give bright yellow; elder gives blues
- heather—gives greeny yellow
- walnuts—soak, unmordanted, in water for 3–4 days for a deep brown
- yew twigs—give reddish pinks

Household waste
- avocado skins—give a range of pinks
- onion skins—give yellows and oranges with alum and copper
- tea bags—give light brown
- beetroot—gives yellow
- turmeric powder—gives orange/yellow
- henna—gives yellows, brownish reds, and very dark brown
- carrots—give yellows
- carrot tops—give a bluish green with a copper mordant
- rhubarb—gives soft yellow/pinks

Dyeing silks, linens, and cottons

In order to get the best quality of color on silks and vegetable fibers such as cotton and linen, there are a few extra processes you can undertake that will ensure good results.

Silk
Dissolve ³/₄ teaspoon of alum in roughly one cup of boiling water and add this to 1 gallon of warm water (no warmer than 98.6°F). Add the thoroughly wetted silk to the warm water, then remove from the heat and allow to soak overnight. Remove the silk from the mordant and rinse thoroughly.

Silk dyes best if you can begin dyeing *immediately* after removing from the mordant bath. *Do not allow the silk to dry before dyeing.* Dye using the same recipes and methods as wool.

Linen and cotton
Pre-mordant as for cotton, using washing soda or gallnuts (see page 70). Then rinse and mordant with alum at 104°F–122°F. Dye as for wool, but double the dyeing time. To keep the intensity of color, only wash in soap-based detergents and finish with a vinegar rinse consisting of 2 teaspoons of white vinegar in a basin of water.

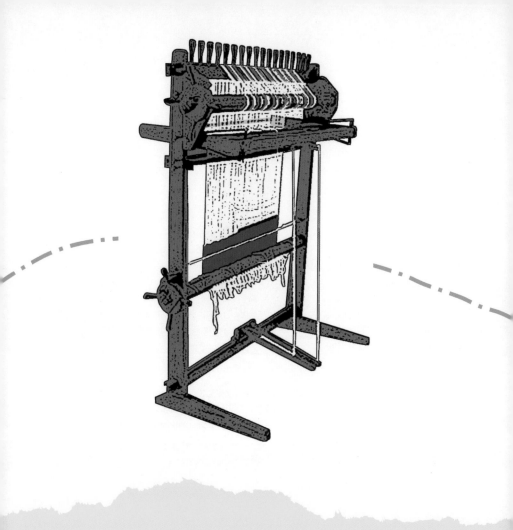

Weaving

Weaving is the process of making cloth by interlacing two sets of threads. The basis of all woven structures is that the horizontal threads—called the weft—interlace with the stationary, often vertical, threads—called the warp. Frames, cards, or looms hold the warp threads in place so that the weft can be easily interlaced over and under them. A loom, which has moving parts, also separates the warp threads so that the weft can be sent across the warp in one movement.

Weaving on a cardboard loom

This method of weaving uses a sheet of cardboard as a simple weaving device. Setting up and weaving on this miniature loom will make some of the possibilities and complications of weaving clearer.

To create the weaving card, take a piece of strong cardboard that will not buckle under tension and cut a zigzag edge at the top and bottom. You can then weave on the card by following these steps:

1) Create the warp by winding a fine two-ply handspun wool or linen (an unplied thread is rarely strong enough) tightly between two of the end zigzags and tie it to itself. Then, keeping the thread under tension, wrap it around and around the card, tying the final wrap to itself again at the end.

2) Using a darning needle, weave a starter thread twice as thick as the warp thread over and under alternate threads of the warp from one side to the other. Then return, going under and over the other alternate threads. You will need about 2 to 4 lines of this thick thread to anchor the warp threads and hold everything together; it doesn't matter what color you use, as it will be turned back or fringed to finish.

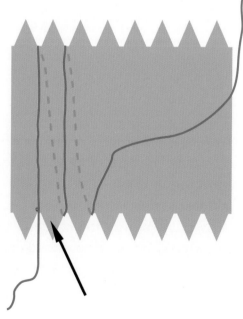

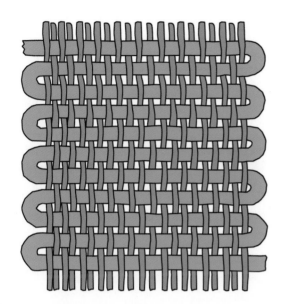

3) Start weaving your square by weaving the thread over and under alternate threads, as you did with the starter thread. You do not need to join this new thread on to the starter thread; the ends can be sewn in later. Each of these rows of weft is called a "pick," and they can be pressed down onto each other with a large kitchen fork.

4) To finish off, weave another two to four rows of thick thread to secure the piece. Then cut the warp threads at the back of the card and carefully remove the card. You can then either knot the warp threads, two together, along the top and bottom of the weaving, or trim the loose warp threads, turn the end of the weaving over, and hem along the edge with wool.

Card weaving is ideal for trying out simple design ideas. It is particularly suitable for children and young people as their fingers are nimble enough to wriggle the threads round the warp and pull them through. They can get rapid results and weave enough to make a small wallet quite quickly.

You can learn a lot from weaving on a card:
• For instance, if you use a weft thread that is the same thickness as the warp, you will see equal amounts of both sets of threads.
• If you use a weft thread that is thicker than the warp and beat the picks down

firmly, they will completely cover the warp threads and form a "weft faced," or tapestry, weave (this is how tapestries are woven, so that the pictures and designs can be seen clearly without the interruptions of the warp).
- If the warp thread is thicker than the weft, the warp will be more obvious and the fabric is known as "warp faced."
- You will be aware that the edges of the weaving are very important, and that if you put the weft thread straight across, the sides will gradually be drawn in because the weft needs an extra allowance at the sides in order to turn around and weave back. To avoid the weaving developing a "waistline," the weft should be passed across the warp in an arc, and not a straight line.
- You will also notice that the edges of the weaving need to be a little stronger than the rest of the fabric and that it is a good idea to have the two or three end warp threads a little closer together than the rest; this is known as a selvedge.

Patterns
You can try some simple but exciting patterns on your card loom.

For horizontal stripes, weave a few centimetres of one color weft thread and then change to another, by pushing the end of one thread through the warp to the back in the middle of a "pick," and starting the next color in the same place, with the end of the thread pushed through to the back of the fabric. Wide and narrow stripes using a weft-faced construction will look just like a tiny carpet.

For vertical stripes, weave one weft pick of one color, followed by one of another color. You will have to wind the two threads round each other at the sides of the fabric and as you repeat this a pattern of vertical stripes will start to appear.

Color and texture. Try out the effects of your handspun, naturally dyed yarns. Perhaps use subtle stripes of different shades, flat silky threads next to fluffy mohairs and alpacas, or very thick two- or three-ply handspun next to finer single threads.

Weaving on a frame

If card weaving is the weaver's sketchbook, the frame is where a full-size painting can be made! A weaving frame can be a sturdy old picture frame with the glass removed and the corners sanded down, or a homemade frame the size of a door, big and strong enough to weave a full-size floor rug or a wall hanging.

Graduating from card to frame you will appreciate the flexibility of being able to weave on warp threads that you can get your fingers around. This means that far more complicated patterns and pictures can be woven and there is much more scope for exploiting your exotic yarns and fine handspun wools. The weaving frame, whatever size or shape, has no moving parts and relies entirely on the weaver's hands to make the patterns and pictures, which gives incredible flexibility to make tiny details but, of course, means that the weaving process is slow.

Making a weaving frame

The alternative to recycling an old picture frame is to make your own weaving frame.

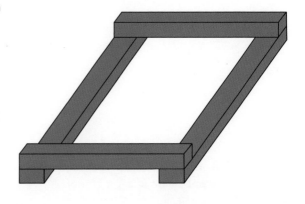

You will need four pieces of wood: top, bottom, and two sides. The top and bottom pieces should be roughly two-thirds the length of the sides. Bear in mind that the longer the sides, the thicker the battens should be to maintain the rigidity of the frame. Place the shorter top and bottom pieces on top of the side pieces, with the corners at right angles, and nail, screw, or glue them in place. Sand down the frame to make sure it is perfectly smooth.

You will also need two or three flat sanded pieces of wood the same width as the warp to act as "shed sticks" or "leashes."

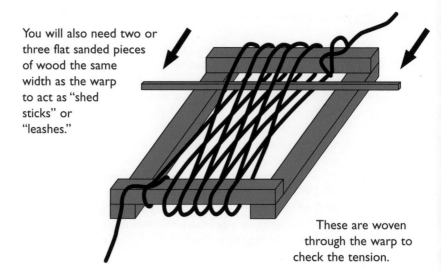

These are woven through the warp to check the tension.

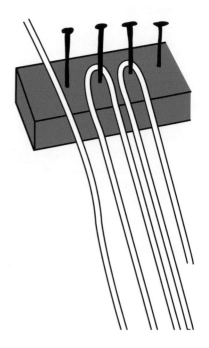

The warp can be attached to the frame either by winding it around the frame or by adding a row of tacks or small nails to the top and bottom pieces to loop the warp threads around.

Threading up a weaving frame

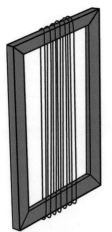

The warp thread on a frame will have to withstand more tension than on a weaving card. The larger the frame, the more tension on the warp, so choose a regular, tightly spun two-ply yarn, wool, or linen.

To thread up a simple frame without nails, tie the warp on at the bottom left-hand side and wrap it around and around the frame lengthways.

Try to wrap the whole warp in one go to keep the tension even. Tie the final end around the frame at the bottom right-hand side. The yarn should be taught with just a bit of give. Group the threads a little nearer together at the edges to strengthen them.

To thread up a frame with nails at the top and bottom, thread the warp in a zigzag from top to bottom of the frame around the nails, moving to the next set of nails each time.

Preparation for weaving on a frame

A row of twining should be added to combine the warp threads and keep them all in place and at the right distance from each other. Using a thread that is three times as thick as the warp thread, weave the twining along the bottom of the warp, leaving the end hanging out. When you reach the end, turn the thread round and wrap over and under the other thread in a figure eight pattern.

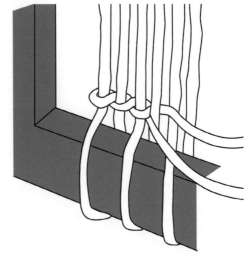

The warp threads should also be checked to ensure that they are of equal tension by weaving a shed stick across, over, and under alternate threads at the top of the frame. This tightens the threads and maintains the tension.

The frame is now your canvas awaiting a picture or pattern. Don't forget that when planning a design you will not be able to weave a piece that is the full size of the frame. Weaving will become very tight from three-quarters of the way up the warp and you will lose 10 percent at the bottom and top when you cut off and finish your weaving.

Weaving on a frame

If you are weaving a picture rather than a repeating pattern where the weft goes right across the warp each time, no more modifications need be made and you can put in three or four rows of a thick, soft starter thread. Leave the end of the thread hanging out at the side; this can be tucked in later. You can then start to weave the weft thread through the warp thread. You will find that you need even more slack on the weft than with the smaller card weaving. Place the weft thread in an arc across the warp, then press down in the middle, making it into an "M" shape—or for a wider warp, press down at two points to make two Ms. Then beat it down horizontally.

Additional tools

If you are making a rug or a piece that will require the weft to go from one side right across to the other side in an unbroken pick, a couple of additional bits of equipment will speed things up.

Shuttle stick: this is a long flat piece of wood with a groove at both ends used for easily pushing the weft thread from one side to the other through alternate threads.

Shed stick with holes: you can make holes at the ends of a flat wooden lath placed horizontally across the warp like the shed stick and weave it into the warp (over and under alternate threads). If you then tie it onto the frame at either side through the holes, you can turn it onto its side, thereby raising up the threads and allowing the shuttle to pass through the "shed" more easily.

Rigid heddle: this tool allows you to lift up one set of alternating threads and then the other. It is rather like a comb that sits across the width of the warp with a hole in each tooth. The warp threads pass alternately through a hole and then between the teeth. When you lift the comb, half of the threads will rise; when you depress the comb below the level of the weaving, it will carry the threads in the holes down, leaving the alternate threads raised. Each time you create a gap through which the shuttle can pass and when you have passed it through the warp, you can then use the comb to bang the weft thread into place. Rigid heddles are cheap to buy from a craft supplier. They are difficult, but not impossible, to make and homemade ones can be customized to the width you require.

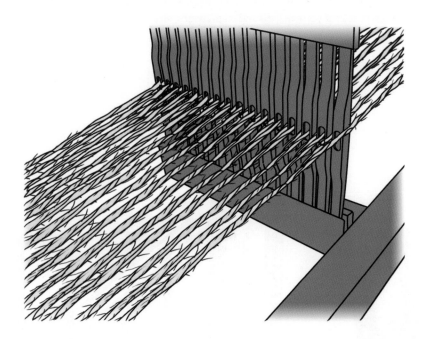

The Brinkley and the peg looms

Before we explore the more complex worlds of tapestry and rug weaving, we should take note of two other weaving methods that are very closely related to frame weaving: the Brinkley loom and the peg loom.

The Brinkley loom
This development of the simple frame solves the problem of threading up a very large frame as it can be fixed to a broom handle and revolved. While keeping the yarn under tension, the frame can be rotated, wrapping the long warp around and around the frame with ease. The Brinkley has its own version of the rigid heddle so that you can lift each set of threads and speed up weaving in the areas where the weft is continuous (i.e., goes from one side right across to the other) or goes across a large part of the warp.

This technique allows large rectangular pieces to be woven very quickly, so it is quite practical to make throws, slip covers, and wraps.

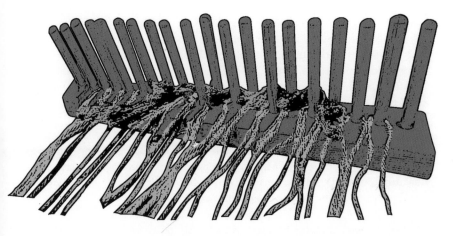

The peg loom

This isn't actually a loom; in fact it is just a row of removable pegs on a timber base. The warp is attached to the pegs by looping lengths of yarn around the pegs or through holes in the pegs. The other ends of the warp lengths can be knotted and weighted to keep them taught. The weft is then wound in and out of the pegs from side to side. When the pegs are filled up to the top with the weft, each peg is lifted out of its hole, pulling the warp with it. The weft is then pushed down onto the hanging warp threads.

This technique is ideal for handspun wools as there are no limitations on the thickness and texture of the yarns. The warp yarns do have to be strong enough to hold the weight of the weft, but otherwise threads can be sausage thick or gossamer fine, blobby or fluffy, or a mixture of yarns. If the pieces are not big enough for purpose, the rectangular pieces can be sewn together.

Tapestry weaving

If you like textiles and spinning, you'll love tapestry weaving. Every thread is part of a picture or design, and color decisions have to be taken every minute. Slow and intricate, the tapestry technique really emphasizes good and bad craftsmanship, and color matching and meticulous care is required with joins and thread ends as mistakes are very obvious.

Tapestry uses a "weft-faced" plain weave (over one and under one) with a "discontinuous" weft, meaning that the weft does not travel from one side of the warp to the other but instead each pattern or pictorial area has its own section of weft. These sections are woven backwards and forwards within the color area and they meet or join other color areas.

When the weft is woven in, it has to be beaten down with either a fork or a tapestry beater, which is like a very heavy wooden fork, and then packed down to cover the warp completely and to create solid picture and pattern areas.

Tapestry uses the simplest sort of loom to make the most complicated sorts of textiles. Setting up a tapestry loom is like warping a frame, as the warp is usually stretched from one beam to the other. The warp should then be spaced with a twining thread and six or ten picks of thick thread should be woven as a starter thread to draw the warp together.

You should set up the design you will be following by either placing a full-scale outline draft on paper and pinning it to the back of the loom behind the warp threads or by painting the design onto the warp in fine black lines. Some weavers can work with the colored design next to the loom and are able to copy and scale it up freehand, but this isn't advisable for beginners!

Attach each color at the place where it falls at the beginning of the design, either wound around a tapestry bobbin or made into a "tapestry butterfly": wound around the fingers and allowing the yarn to gently pull out as it weaves in (see picture, right).

The areas of different colored weft can be joined together in a great number of ways.

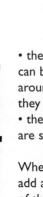

For example:
- the different colors can be wound around each other where they meet (see right);
- the wefts threads can be looped around the same thread that they are joining;
- the edges of colored areas can be stepped so that there is no split in the warp (see below);

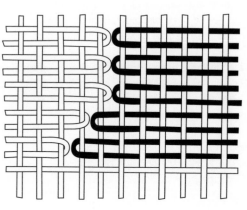

- the different colored threads can be wound alternately around the warp threads where they meet;
- they can be left as slits that are sewn up later.

When the tapestry is complete, add another three or four picks of thicker yarn and a double row of twining to hold the weaving together.

Using leashes

Tapestry looms mostly depend on the finger manipulation of the weaver to wriggle the weft through the warp but this can be aided by a system of "leashes" to separate the warp threads. Leashes are loops of thread that wrap around alternate warp threads and are tied around the "leash rod" at the top of the loom. When a group of threads has to be lifted to create a weaving space, a group of leashes can be pulled down and the weft passed through using the fingers or a tapestry bobbin.

Tips for tapestry weaving

• Be especially vigilant of the edges of the weaving where the thick, heavy weft wraps around the much finer warp. The weft threads should wind neatly round the outer warp threads, neither pulling them in nor leaving loops.

• It may be necessary to tye the edge of the weaving onto the side of the frame at intervals to prevent distortion. This is called "bracing."

• Although most traditional tapestries were woven using a weft yarn of uniform thickness, mixed thicknesses and textures of handspun yarn can look very effective. However, in order to prevent distortion, an area of thicker yarn will have to be matched by more picks in an area of thin yarn.

• Traditionally, tapestry warps were multiple plys of fine linen singles spun "S" (counterclockwise) and plied the same way. The linen was spun and plied with wet fibers and the skeins dried under extreme tension. This can be done and creates a smooth, shiny tapestry warp but it is not easy and takes a lot of time!

• Hand spinning the warp yarn for a tapestry is not for the beginner as beating down the weft exposes the warp yarn to a lot of friction.

Rug weaving on a large frame

Rugs are generally for the floor and so
need to be very strong. For this reason,
rug looms are strong and husky.

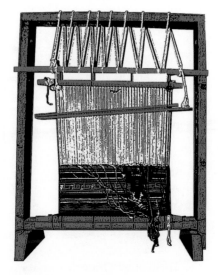

Rug weaving is just a bigger, thicker
version of weaving on a frame. The warp
threads can be attached to the loom by
either winding them right round the
frame or by winding the warp thread
round hooks or nails at the top and
bottom. The warp will have to be
spaced at a maxium of 6–7 ends per
inch to allow for the thicker yarn in the
weft to be pressed down. Long shuttle
sticks will have to be used to push the
weft across the wider warp. One or
two shed sticks are useful to keep the warp tension even. Weaving is the same
process as on a tapestry frame, but a heavy kitchen fork or specialized "rug
beater" is needed to bash the weft into place.

Rug looms often have two shafts: one to lift one half of alternate threads
across the warp and one to lift the other ones. This means that the weaver
can make a plain weave without handling the warp at all by weaving the weft
yarn from side to side. Some rug looms have weights at the bottom to hold
the warp taught during weaving.

There is no reason why rug weaving techniques can't be used on a homemade
frame loom or a Brinkley to make a flat weave or a pile rug.

Rugs can be woven in a simple flat plain weave, but pile (the yarns that stand
up or out from the weave) can be added (either all over or just in places) by
using several methods.

Soumac weave

This weave gives a smooth pile surface. The wool weft is taken forwards over four threads, then down through the warp and back under two threads, then forward again over four, like stem stitch embroidery. Alternate rows of Soumac are worked in the opposite direction and two rows of Soumac are separated by two rows of plain weave.

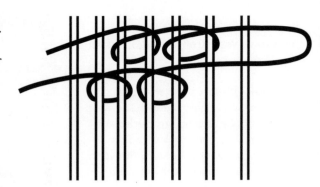

Turkish or Ghiordes knots

This is slow but great fun! After every two plain picks the warp is followed by a row of knots. The knots are made by cutting the wool into short pieces, which are doubled and looped through the warp and knotted in pairs from left to right. After 10 to 12 in. has been woven the pile can be trimmed. Don't forget the selvedge, which has to be worked up to an equal height to the weaving by adding a few rows to it each time.

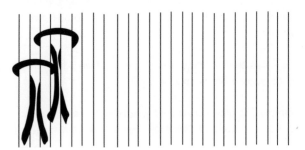

The ends of the rug can be knotted in various border patterns.

Taking rugs and tapestries off the loom

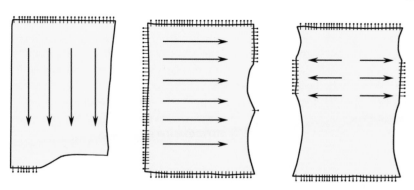

All cloth, rugs, and tapestries should be finished with at least 1 ½ or 2 in. of plain weave in the warp yarn, more for a heavy hanging or rug, and less for a tiny piece of weaving for a wallet or placemat.

If you are removing a rug or tapestry from a frame or Brinkley loom, you will have lots of unwoven warp. Cut through the back warp threads and take down the tapestry. The bottom threads may have been looped around nails so ease them off. Place the weaving face down on a clean bedsheet on the floor (or a table). Trim the warp threads, leaving a good length for finishing off.

First the fabric should be "mended." This means stitching in all the loose ends that you put to the back of the fabric during weaving. With a needle, thread up each tail and run it back into the weave and down one of the warp threads. When it is tucked in far enough, snip it off near the weaving.

Blocking
Hand woven fabrics, especially heavy tapestries and rugs, will not be rectangular when they come off the loom, especially if they are woven from handspun yarn. The tensions of twist and weaving has to be settled by a process called "blocking." The best way to do this is on a large board covered with a blanket and plastic sheet.

Pin down one side of your weaving and stroke the other side so that it is lined up with the other side of the board at its fullest extent, keeping the warp completely straight in the weave direction. Then pin down one selvedge edge and stroke the other out to its fullest extent and pin down. You now have your fabric stretched into the perfect rectangle. I would not recommend pressing or steaming fabric made from handspun yarn, which may still have the character of the fleece imprinted within it. Either dampen the fabric with a sponge or spray it with a light water spray; this will be enough to set the fabric. When it is dry it will retain a perfect rectangle without flattening the surface of your fabric, taking away attractive irregularities.

Finishing your woven piece

Finishing and decorative fringe effects are as important as any other aspect of successful textile making. A good finish or a sumptuous fringe can make handmade textiles look much more professional and drape more beautifully as well as displaying fabulously colored handspun yarns to advantage. Until your tapestry has a border so that it can be hung on the wall, or your wraps and throws have a fringe or woven edge, they are just samples and can't really be used, and are in fact in danger of falling apart. There are lots of simple methods for easily adding the finishing touch that will enhance the qualities of your home-produced textiles.

Finishing by teasling

Traditional finishing and scouring processes are not really necessary for hand woven pieces made from homespun wool. The wool has been washed and set after spinning so it is no longer in the grease (which is how wool was traditionally woven). Thoroughly washing the handspun woolen yarn should also have preshrunk it and the final blocking should ensure that the woven piece keeps its shape. If the fleece was a very soft breed or if you have mixed in some kid mohair or Angora rabbit you might wish to raise the "nap" (fluff the fabric up a little) to make a cuddly rug or cot blanket. The best and gentlest way of doing this is to use the head of a teasle plant to gently stroke the fabric in short strokes. If you are fluffing a large blanket and want to speed up the process, you can tape strong cardboard over the teeth of a wool carder and tape several teasle heads to that.

Twisted fringe

There are a number of different methods for making fringes. The most suitable for light fabrics is a twisted fringe; it works especially well on handwoven silk scarves or light wool stoles.

1) Weave the item, leaving 4 to 6 in. of unwoven warp at the end or ends where you want fringes.
2) Take three warp ends and twist them to the right until the yarn begins to kink.
3) Holding on to these yarns, take the next three warp yarns and twist in the same direction again until they begin to kink.
4) Hold the two bundles of three yarns together and let them twist to the left around each other. They will twist into one fringe.
5) Tie the end in a small neat knot around itself.
6) Move across the shawl or scarf and repeat steps 2 to 5 until all the ends are fringed. If you don't have an even number of threads, you can make a few fringes with less or more threads in them.

Diamond pattern fringe

Diamond pattern knotting is suitable for heavier warp but also looks good in a soft wool or worsted yarn.

1) Weave the item, leaving a good length of yarn at the end or ends where you want fringes.
2) Tie the ends of the warp in knots, in groups of four or six yarns.
3) Part one bunch of yarn in half, moving the left half to the side diagonally.
4) Place a weaving hook on top of the left yarn.
5) Part the yarn on the next bunch to the left and put the right half of the yarn on top of the hook.
6) Loop the second lot of yarn underneath and around the hook and first yarn.
7) Catch the top of the second yarn in the hook and pull them through the loop to create a knot.
8) Continue knotting the yarn from adjacent bunches until they are all knotted.
9) Now split the new bunches in half and tie them in the same way to create a diamond pattern.

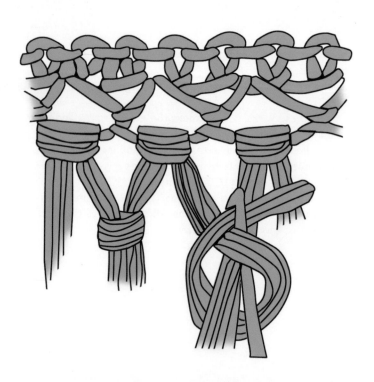

Woven fringe

This method of fringing has to be anticipated before starting the weaving.
After several rows of plain weave, a flat shed stick double the width of the
fringe should be woven through the warp. Then weaving should be continued
on the other side of the flat stick. Another stick should be put in at the other
end of the weaving and the weaving continued around this stick. When the
woven piece is cut off the loom and the sticks are
removed, there will be gap of just warp threads
where the sticks were. These warps should then be
folded in half and hemmed together so the warp
threads form loops. Finally, the turned-up loops of
warp should be cut into a fringe.

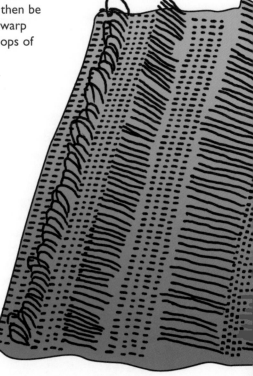

Weft yarn fringe

To make a fringe from weft yarn, first hem the end rows of plain weave and turn them up to make a solid edge to the weaving. Then take a separate length of the yarn you have used for the weft and wind it around a piece of card, then cut it into small lengths. The pieces of weft yarn can then be folded in half and attached to the turned-under edge of the weaving by pulling the folded loop through with a hook and securing it with a double hitch (lark's head) knot. You can then knot the fringe in bunches if you like.

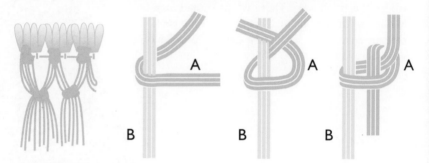

Chain or macramé fringes

This fringing is made of very long lengths of weft yarn cut to size. The folded lengths should be looped around the end of the weaving in pairs and secured with a double hitch knot to give four lengths of yarn. The outside pair are then knotted around the middle two, and then knotted again to make a square knot. The chain of knots can then continue down or the group of four can be linked to the next group, giving a macramé border. This works best in a stiff warp yarn.

Woven edges

This edging makes and finishes the weaving without the need for hemming. It makes a neat, stiff finish for a heavy tapestry that has been woven on a linen warp. Based on the ancient method of "finger weaving," which preceded weaving with any looms, it is also a method of making braids or strips.

Weave the item, leaving a good length of unwoven warp at one or both ends. Take eight warp ends at the side of the warp and push the woven edge in a straight line firmly up the threads into the weaving. The first warp thread on the left side then becomes a weft and is taken over and under each of the other seven warps until it comes to the end of the group of eight. Now take the second thread and make the same journey over and under the warp threads, including a ninth warp thread at the end. Push the second thread behind the threads. This is repeated with all of the threads, moving across the warp until the last few threads at the right hand side; these are then either stitched back up into the weaving or plaited into a neat little tail.

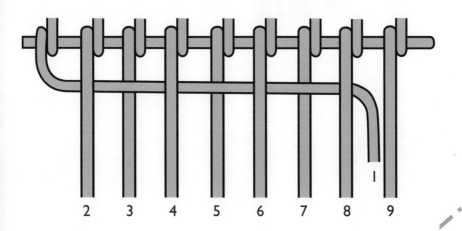

Projects

These four projects have been made in the most self-sufficient manner possible, using only manual power, natural color, and materials obtained at very little expense or for nothing. They may give some ideas for making simple but usable textiles that will involve some of the processes covered in previous chapters. Descriptions of the spinning, weaving, knitting, and finishing processes used are included, along with an indication of amounts of fiber and dyestuffs.

Striped frame-woven cushion cover

As cushions can be any shape or size, the dimensions of your woven cushion cover can be dictated by the size of your weaving frame. For example, a large picture frame will give enough weaving area to make a moderately-sized cushion cover. The front and back of the cover do not need to match and so all sorts and colors of yarn can be used up to make the weaving bright and colorful.

Amount
The quantity of yarn will depend on the size of frame you are using. To find out the length of yarn needed, measure the length of the frame from top to bottom and multiply this by the number of threads you will put on as warp. Double this if the warp is to be wrapped right around the frame.

Spinning
Use a firmly twisted, smoothly spun wool for the warp. It is best to use wool from sheep with a longer fleece and spin from combed slivers. To create a striped effect, you will need various different colors of yarn for the weft; these can be any type of wool and any colors you choose. Thicker yarns will give raised areas and finer yarns will give flat or transparent areas.

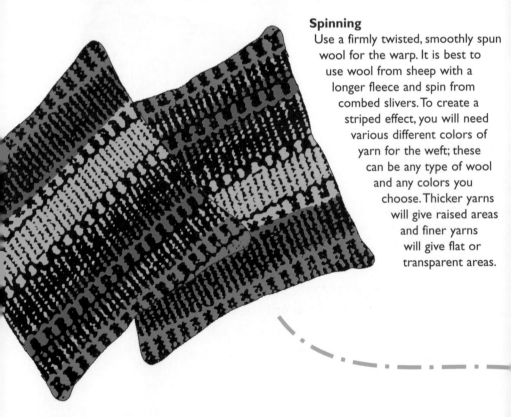

Weaving

Wind the warp onto the frame, then chain a thick doubled thread along the bottom to keep the warp threads in place. Then weave two or three rows of a yarn that is thicker than the warp yarn, by lifting the alternate warp threads with the fingers, pushing the weft through with a shuttle and banging the weft into place with a heavy kitchen fork. This will give a plain weave.

Changing the weft yarns after several rows will automatically result in horizontal stripes. Let the end of the previous color hang out at the side of the weaving—it can be sewn or tucked in as part of the finishing process—and commence the next color, leaving the end of that color hanging out at the side as well. If you have only very small amounts of handspun dyed yarn, even samples or experiments, you can weave them across for a weft row or two; it will add to the pattern.

Weaving alternate colored threads will give stripes of little vertical lines between the broader stripes. In the image shown, a small amount of black has been woven from right to left, then a small amount of white from left to right, followed by black and then white, and so on.

When you get to the top of the frame or the place where the warp becomes too tight to weave any more, put in another one or two rows of a thicker thread.

Finishing

Turn the frame over and place on a clean cloth. Sew or weave in all the ends at the sides of the weaving. If there are lots of stripes there will be lots of ends hanging out. Take the warp threads that have been at the back and cut them in the middle. Use these long threads to make a woven finishing edge (see page 109). Then trim the long threads off.

Repeat the weaving and finishing process again to make another woven rectangle. Then sew the two pieces of weaving together inside out, making sure to sew in all the loose weft ends at the sides.

Ribbed alpaca hat

Handspun alpaca will knit into wonderfully warm winter hats, gloves, and scarves. Alpaca also comes in more natural colors than any other fiber or wool, and this knitted hat uses these natural shades to make a three-color effect.

Amount
5$^1/_3$ oz. raw alpaca fleece will reduce to 3$^1/_2$ oz. yarn after discarding bits in the fleece and short, tangled hairs. Start off with 1$^3/_4$ oz. white fleece, 1$^3/_4$ oz. blond/fawn fleece, and 1$^3/_4$ oz. brown fleece.

Combing
Hand tease out all the fleece, then comb with a dog comb or flick carder for spinning.

Spinning
Spin a loose, soft thread with each color, then ply into two-ply. The finished two-ply should be the thickness that will wrap round a ruler at 4 ends per $^3/_8$ in. Make one ball each of each shade.

Knitting
To find out if the yarn is the right thickness and that the tension of the stitches is correct, a sample square of spun two-ply thread should be knitted before all the yarn is spun. Cast on 10 stitches and knit 10 rows in knit, 2 pearl, 2 rib. Adjust the rest of the spinning if this doesn't measure 2 in. square.

On a size 10 circular needle, cast on 70 stitches in white alpaca. Knit 2, pearl 2 until the color is used up, then join in the blond alpaca and knit until that is used up. Finally join in brown. Continue until the hat is long enough to reach the top of your head (you can pull it on holding the circular needle). Then knit 10, knit 2 together for the next row.

Next row: knit 9, knit 2 together.

Next row: knit 8, knit 2 together, and so on until the last remaining few stitches so you end up with 2 stitches.

Sew the yarn in on the crown and add a pompom on top if you wish.

Tie-dye rug

You can create lovely tie-dyed effects on your yarn by dipping tied and wrapped skeins into dyes. A peg loom is a fast way to weave a large textile item, as setting up is so quick in comparison with a horizontal loom, where every single warp yarn has to be threaded through.

Amount
The warp will need 1 lb. 3½ oz. linen yarn. The measurement of the yarn is $^6/_{10}$ leas, a medium-fine linen that will have to be bought unless you want a real challenge and hand spin it. The weft should be spun from 2 lbs. 3 oz. of a medium-weight fleece, such as Portland fleece.

Carding
Card the wool into rolags. If you have access to a drum carder, card this large quantity into batts.

Spinning
Spin into single-ply yarn. For this project the exact width of the yarn does not matter. Wind the yarn into skeins and wash thoroughly.

Dyeing
First rewind the skeins of weft yarn so that they are the exact width of the warp you will put on the peg loom. Prepare 4 lbs. 6 oz. of chopped woad. Pour on boiling water and add ammonia or urine. Whisk and add sodium dithionite, thiourea dioxide (which can be purchased as Spectralite), or any reducing agent. Bind the edges of the skeins tightly with string, then wrap in cloth.

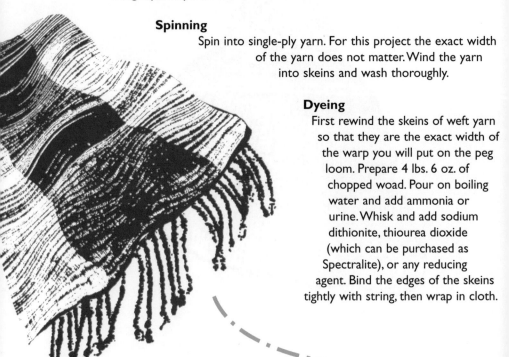

Immerse the center of the skeins in the dye, leaving edges undyed. Then aerate and repeat four times. Rinse in a sink of water with two tablespoons of white vinegar and then wash in soapy water until the water runs clear.

Weaving
Warp up the peg loom with doubled linen threads, each 4 ft. 11 in. long. Weave doubled singles through the pegs, making sure that the woad-dyed area sits in the middle of the weaving. The blue parts of each pick should lie just above the previous blue area.

Finishing
When the rug is 3 ft. $^1/_3$ in. long, knot the warp threads together in threes at the bottom, remove from the peg loom at the top, and knot in threes. Plait the fringe in threes and knot each plait. Wash in warm water, if you like (inevitably, the blue will bleed into the white slightly), then brush the surface of the rug until a halo of fluff stands off it.

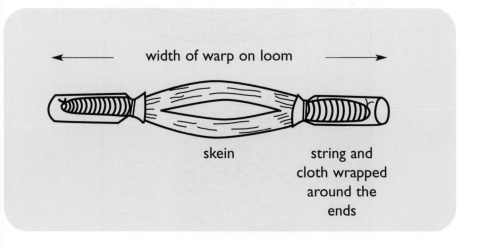

width of warp on loom

skein

string and
cloth wrapped
around the
ends

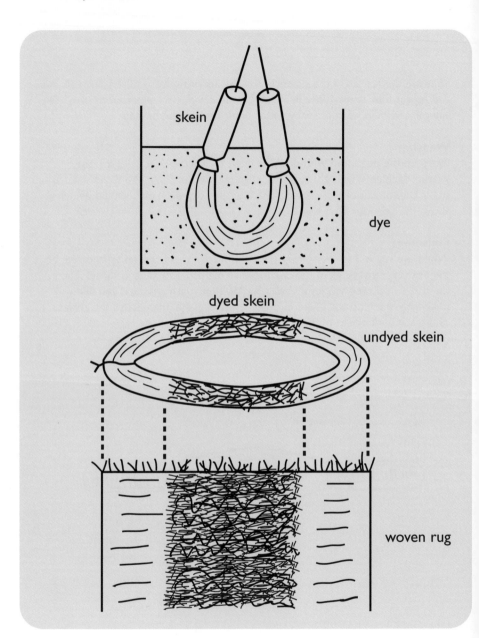

Chunky scarf

This is a project that will use up leftover
bits of handspun yarn. Unspun fleece and
carded bits can also be woven in.

Amount
For the weft, use 2^1/$_2$ oz. of leftover wool, mohair
or alpaca. For the warp, use 1^3/$_4$ oz. merino wool.

Carding
Card the weft mixture into batts on the drum carder, and
hand card the merino into rolags.

Spinning
Spin the drum-carded sheets into chunky, random yarn, using a drop
spindle (as the irregularities will make the yarn too fat for the orifice of the
spinning wheel). Spin the merino fleece into 1 oz. of two-ply yarn. The width
of the yarn should be 5 threads to ^{3}/$_8$ in. when wound around a ruler.

Dyeing
Mordant all the yarn in either a copper mordant made from a copper
bracelet or cook in rhubarb to mordant (see pages 68 and 71).
Then make up two dye baths of any of the dye plants you have in
the garden and divide the skeins of yarn between them.

Weaving
Make a narrow warp on a frame with the fine wool—
approximately three ends per ^{3}/$_8$ in. Weave a little of the
finer wool as a starter, then weave in the random yarn.
You can include pieces of unspun fleece or rovings.
Pull the lumps in the random yarn to the surface to
accentuate the texture. Finish with some rows of
fine wool.

Finishing

If you want a fluffy scarf, dampen and brush thoroughly with a carder to raise the surface. Fringe the warp threads however you like (see pages 105–8).

Resources

For further information on fibers and for spinning, dyeing, and weaving supplies, please visit these Web sites:

American Sheep Industry Association
www. sheepusa.org/Home

National Angora Rabbit Breeders Club
www.nationalangorarabbitbreeders.com

Eastern Angora Goat and Mohair Association
www.angoragoats.com/marketplace.html

Mohair Council of America
www.mohairusa.com

Alpacas in the USA!
www.alpacasintheusa.com

Keep The Fleece
www.keepthefleece.org

AgriSeek—World's Largest Marketplace
www.agriseek.com/buy/e/Ag-Products/Animal-Fiber

For Farmers
www.forfarmers.com/sell-buy/e/Products/Fiber/Other

For links to supplies, please visit: www.einet.net/directory/48221/Supplies.htm

Glossary

Batts   carded sheets of fibers.

Carding   preparing wool for spinning by brushing it between two flat carders.

Combing   preparing wool for spinning by separating the fibers using a comb.

Count   the wool count is a measure of the size of woolen yarn.

Crimp   the curl or wave in wool.

Decoction   water in which vegetable matter has been boiled until the constituents of the vegetable make a soup.

Drum carder   a machine with a revolving cylinder that arranges wool fibers into batts.

Guard Hairs   long coarse wool hairs that protect the soft under-fleece.

Hackling   the combing and splitting of flax fibers.

Indican   a chemical in certain plants that gives indigo dye.

Kemp   coarse, thick, whitish hairs in a sheep's fleece.

Lazy Kate   a rack used to hold bobbins when plying yarn.

Lea(s)   the unit of measure for linen thread.

Mordant   a substance that enables dye to become fixed onto fibers.

Niddy-noddy   a wooden stick with shorter cross sticks at the top and bottom. It is used to wind yarn into a skein.

Pic   one weft thread woven across the warp.

Ply   to join together strands of yarn by twisting them together.

Rigid heddle   a rectangular piece of wood or metal that fits across the warp. Alternate splits and holes have the warp yarns threaded through them and enable alternate threads to be lifted and depressed.

Rolag	a sausage-shaped cylinder of wool. Spinning from a rolag is quicker and makes a better thread.
"S" threads	threads twisted in a counterclockwise direction.
Scutching	breaking up the stems of dried flax to release the fibers.
Selvedge	the edging of a piece of cloth, which prevents unraveling.
Shed stick	a flat piece of wood that is woven over and under the warp threads to maintain tension.
Shuttle stick	a long stick with weft yarn wound round it, which is used to push the weft through the warp.
Sliver	a combed length of wool with parallel threads.
Solar box	a box with one glass side that catches sunlight to use it for energy.
Spindle	a length of wood or metal used to twist fibers into yarn.
Staple	a lock of sheep's wool.
Staple length	the average length of all the staples in fleece.
Starter thread	the length of spun thread that is already around the spindle or bobbin, to which new fibers can be attached.
Warp	the threads stretched lengthways across a loom or frame, across which the weft is woven.
Weft	the threads woven at right angles across the warp threads.
Whorl	the disc on a spindle or bobbin that increases the rotation.
Woolen	yarn made from wool by carding into cylindrical rolags and spinning.
Worsted	yarn made from wool by combing it into slivers and spinning.
"Z" threads	threads twisted in a clockwise direction.

A
alpaca 10, 13, 27–28
  Ribbed alpaca hat
  114–15
Angora goats 11, 26–27
Angora rabbits 10, 13,
  28, 54

B
Brinkley loom 96

C
Cashmere goats 12, 27
cats 14
Chunky scarf 119–20
combing and carding
  31–41
  drum carding 39–40
  hand carding 36–38
cotton 29, 41
  dyeing 85
craft suppliers 19
crimp 23, 28

D
decoction 63–64
doffing 38
dogs 14
dyeing 59–85
  black 83
  blue 5–78
  equipment 65–66
  golden yellow 81–82

grow your own color
  60–61
harvesting and storing
  plants 62–63
natural dyes 61–62
plants 61
process 63
recipes for dye plants
  72–84
red and pink 72–74
silks, linen, and cotton
  85
yellow and orange
  78–80

E
eBay 20
energy efficiency 68

F
fiber 9–29
  exotic animal fibers 29
  recycled 18
  sourcing and choosing
  wool and fleeces
  19–29
  vegetable 16–18, 29, 41
  waste 29
flax 41
fringes
  chain or macramé 08
  diamond pattern 106
  twisted 105

weft yarn 108
woven 107

G
gifts 20

H
hackling 41
haybox 66–67
hemp 17, 29, 41

K
kemp 23
knitting or blanket wool
  57

L
"Lazy Kate" 53
linen 16, 29
  and silk weaving thread
  57
  dyeing 85
  spinning 54

M
merino and angora
  knitting wool 57
mohair 26–27
  spinning 54
mordant/mordanting 63,
  64–65
  recipes for mordants
  68–71

N
nettle 41
  fiber 17–18
niddy-noddy 55

P
peg loom 97

R
ramie nettle 29
rare breed farms 19–20
Ribbed alpaca hat
  114–15
rigid heddle 95

S
scouring 23
scutching 41
selvedges 104
shed stick 94
sheep 10
  and wool festivals 20
  longwool and luster 21
  mountain and
    moorland 21
  shortwool and
    downland breeds 21
shuttle stick 94
silk 28
  dyeing 75
  spinning 54
silkworms 14–15

solar box 67
spinning 43–57
  drop spindle 46, 47–48
  finger 44
  linen 54
  mohair 54
  plying on the wheel 53
  preparing vegetable
    fibers 41
  silk 54
  skeining handspun yarn
    55
  spindle 44, 46
  using a spinning wheel
    50
  woolen 52–53
staple length 32
  measuring 23
"S" threads 48
Striped frame-woven
  cushion cover 112–13

T
tapestry
  weaving 97
  yarn 57
teasing 32
teasling 104–105
Tie-dye rug 116–17

W
weaving 87–109
  blocking 103

card 88–90
frame 91–95
rug 101–103
Soumac weave 102
tapestry 97–100
Turkish or Ghiordes
  knots 102
wool
  plying 49
  staplers 19
worsted 33, 53
woven edges 109

Y
yarn
  designing 57
  fancy twisted wool 57
  tapestry 57
  washing 56–57, 64

Z
"Z" threads 48

Acknowledgments

My thanks to the editors of this book (Corinne Masciocchi and Louise Coe) for their diligence and patience. Grateful thanks also to the spinning group at Vauxhall City Farm in central London, for their enthusiasm, help, and willingness to experiment with self-sufficient textile projects.